From the Author of *Feels Like The First Time*

Both Sides Now

Shawn Inmon

with Dawn Inmon

Both Sides Now
By Shawn Inmon

❧

©2013 by Shawn Inmon

Cover Design: Linda Boulanger
    www.TellTaleBookCovers.weebly.com
Interior Design: Ellen Sallas, The Author's Mentor
    www.theauthorsmentor.com

Published by Pertime Publishing

Also available in eBook publication

Dedication

*This book is dedicated to Sheilah Galpin, Bonnie
Powell and Jessica Coen.
When things were dark, you were the light.*

This is a True Story

Just When I Needed You Most

February 1979

The instruction sheet had said not to eat breakfast. That was good advice, because when Dad turned into the parking lot of the Planned Parenthood building, I started to feel sick to my stomach. He found a parking spot by the front door of the building, turned to Mom and said, "I'll wait here."

She nodded at him, and we got out and sloshed through the puddles and rain to reach the double glass doors. There was a waiting room inside, with uncomfortable chairs and benches and a lady sitting behind a desk. A rack held pamphlets with helpful titles like *Sex and the Adolescent*. If I hadn't been so queasy, I might have laughed at that. Instead I couldn't manage anything but a grimace.

Mom walked up to the lady behind the desk and said, "We have an appointment. It will be under Dawn Welch."

The lady checked her appointment log, nodded, and handed Mom a clipboard with some forms. "Fill these out, please." Mom sat down and scribbled for a few minutes, then handed me the clipboard and a wad of money. I took both up to the lady behind the desk and handed them to her.

"Just a moment. I'll get your receipt."

I said "Thank you," sat down, closed my eyes and pretended I was somewhere else. Anywhere else. I was afraid I was going to throw up all over the clean tile floor.

A few minutes later, a nurse in a white uniform opened a door and said, "Dawn? Dawn Welch?"

Never Going Back Again
December 1, 2006

For as long as I could remember, life had been a merry-go-round that never slowed down enough for me to catch my balance. I had separated from my husband Rick a few years earlier. Since then, life had gotten better, but things were still hard. I worked two jobs, trying to keep me and my daughters Connie and Dani afloat. Even with two jobs, we were slipping below the waves. The worst part of every day was going to the mailbox. I was behind on the mortgage on our little house and the bank was constantly threatening to foreclose. I paid my utility bill every month the day before it was shut off. If we lost the house, I didn't know where we would go next. My mom and dad had both passed away and I didn't have any other family nearby.

I worked as a Supervisor at a Call Center for ACS in Tumwater. As a Supervisor, I had two jobs. One part I loved: I trained a team of twelve agents to be as successful as they could be. They handled calls from people that were unhappy about their Verizon Wireless bills. You can imagine how much fun that was. It was when a customer was really angry that the part I didn't like came: Supervisor calls. I knew eventually I would have as much as I could take and I would tell some customer exactly what I thought. No doubt, that would be my last Supervisor call and my last day working for ACS.

In the evenings and on my day off, I moonlighted part-time at a little hamburger stand in Centralia called Bill & Bea's. The work was pretty boring, but Connie worked there too. No matter how bad things were, she could make me laugh. I liked working at B&B's, mostly because it meant I got to spend time with

Connie.

On December 1st, I got up at 4 AM and worked a full shift at ACS. I was exhausted and daydreaming about taking a nap before my shift at Bill & Bea's that night. Sometimes the promise of a nap is what got me through my shift. It rarely happened, and today was no exception. Something always needed to be done.

By 8:30 that night, I was pretty much dead on my feet, but there was still half an hour before closing time. As Connie and I were starting our closing procedures, making sure everything was cleaned, filled and ready for the next day, another car pulled up to the drive-through window.

I was filling the sugar dispensers on the counter, so Connie opened the window and took the order. I heard a man order a chicken sandwich and a Coke. I was glad he didn't have a huge order that would make us late getting out of there. As tired as I was, I had a date to go to the new casino in Rochester. I wasn't excited about the guy, but I was kind of over needing to be excited about a guy before I went out with him. Anyway, a trip to the casino sounded like more fun than wiping down countertops and filling ketchup bottles, or being called terrible names by someone who hadn't monitored his kid's cell phone usage and wanted to curse someone else for it.

"Hey, Mom," I heard Connie call from behind the grill. "I forgot to ask him if he wanted onions on his sandwich. Will you check?"

I slid the window open and leaned out. The driver looked like he was in his mid-forties, with short brown hair, resembling about a hundred other guys that came through the drive-through every day.

"Do you want onions on your sandwich?" I asked.

For some reason, this relatively easy question didn't seem to register with him. He blinked and opened his mouth like he was going to answer, but nothing came out. Finally, he managed one word: "Huh?"

I slowed my speech down for him a little bit, in case he was, well, slow.

"I just need to know if you want onions on your sandwich."

After another long moment, he finally stuttered, "Yeah, sure."

We made all our food fresh to order, so it took time for

Connie to make his sandwich and cook his fries. She noted that the slow-witted driver was staring at us. The customers could see right into the kitchen from the drive-through, but when the window was closed, they couldn't hear us.

"We've got another one, Mom," Connie said. "I think he likes you."

For some reason, a lot of guys think the drive-through is the perfect place to launch their pickup lines.

"Yeah, well, I think he's kinda cute."

"Eww, gross, Mom. He's old!"

I laughed. Eighteen-year-old girls don't think any guy in his forties can be cute, other than maybe Johnny Depp. I looked at him more closely and saw that he had his left hand out the window, with a wedding ring on it. Whatever interest I had in flirting with him evaporated.

I took his sandwich and fries and put them in a brown bag, folding the top over so the food would stay warm if he didn't eat it right away. I slid the window open and handed it through to him.

"That'll be $8.66, please."

He looked a little dazed, but gave me a half-smile and handed me a ten-dollar bill. When I gave him his change, he had an odd expression on his face, like he'd seen a ghost.

"Did you go to Mossyrock High School?" he asked.

"Yes..."

"Class of '82?"

"No, Class of '81." I stared at him harder, trying to place him. It wasn't unusual for someone I went to school with to recognize me at the drive-through, since we weren't that far from Mossyrock, but most people who did were a year or two behind me. He didn't look like any of the underclassmen I could remember.

He eased the car forward, like he was going to just drive off. I wasn't about to let him get away that easy. "And you are...?"

"We went to school together," he said.

I searched my memory but I was coming up blank. I gave a small shake of my head, feeling a little helpless. I hated it when someone recognized me and I had no clue who they were.

"Dawn, it's Shawn."

I could tell he thought that would end the mystery, but it

didn't. Maybe it was the exhaustion of having been awake for nineteen hours, but whatever the reason, I wasn't making a connection. I bit the inevitable bullet.

"Shawn who?"

That struck home. He had clearly expected me to remember him, but I just didn't.

"Shawn Inmon. We lived next door to each other..."

I don't know if he kept talking after that, because I wasn't able to hear any more. There was a sudden ocean's-roar in my ears that blocked out everything else.

Shawn.

I had buried everything about Shawn so deep that I was sure it would never resurface. I thought I would never see him again. Now here he was, right in front of me. The last I heard, he was married, had kids, and had moved away. His mom had never missed a chance to tell me he was happy. Memories and emotions churned through me, and I was helpless to stop them.

I took a step back and my hands flew to my mouth.

"Oh my God. Oh. My. God. OhmyGod."

Somewhere deep inside, I knew I was losing it, but I knew that from a distance, watching myself freak out. I couldn't speak. I couldn't move. I couldn't do anything. I was vaguely aware that Shawn was still talking, but I couldn't hear what he was saying. That rushing noise in my ears was blocking out everything else.

Out of the corner of my eye, I saw Connie walk over and smile at Shawn. He was talking to her. *Shawn is talking to Connie. Does he think she's his? If he does the math, he should know she's not.* I was rooted to one spot, chanting "Oh my God." I didn't know if I would ever be able to stop repeating that. Memories flooded through me. I remembered laughing, talking, playing catch in our yard. I remembered dancing barefoot after Prom, soft kisses and feeling so safe in his arms. I was always safe when I was with him. Then I remembered that he left. He left and never came back.

I had tried to locate him off and on over the years, but I never found him. I didn't want to talk to him, mostly because I didn't want him to know how my life had turned out, but I wanted to know where he was and if he was doing well.

He and Connie eventually finished whatever conversation they were having, and I saw his car ease forward. He took one last look at me over his shoulder before he turned right onto Harrison, headed toward I-5.

"Mom, are you OK?"

I looked at Connie and finally found the 'off' switch for the constant repetition of "Oh my God." I nodded a little, but was having a hard time focusing.

"Who was that?" Connie asked.

"That was my first." Connie's eyes widened. I didn't have to explain.

My brain started to work again. He had said, "We went to school together." Was that all I was to him? A classmate he left behind while he went on to bigger and better things?

"We went to school together," I mumbled, shaking my head. "I guess Mom was right. I can't believe that's all I was to him."

I still had salt and pepper shakers to fill and tables to wipe down while Connie cleaned the grill. I was supposed to meet the guy who was taking me to the casino in just a few minutes, but I had forgotten all about him.

All I could think about was the feeling I'd had when Shawn and I were together. I should have been getting ready to go, but I felt like I was stuck in the 70s.

Oh, Very Young

My life story was almost very short. I was born in Torrance Memorial Hospital in Torrance, California on December 27th, 1963. A lot of things about my birth are still mysteries to me, but I know I arrived with quite a few health problems. At first, the doctors diagnosed me with a heart defect. They were wrong about that, but I had other issues for them to deal with. The woman I eventually came to know as my mom told me many years later that my birth mother died giving birth to me. Like so many things, I don't know if that was legend or truth.

What I do know is that I was given to Colleen and Burt Decker as a foster child when I was three weeks old. The state wouldn't allow me to be adopted because I was so sickly. I think they were trying to save Mom the expense and heartache of adopting a baby girl who was just going to die anyway. Happily, the state was incorrect, and Mom legally adopted me in 1967. We lived in a little three-bedroom house on a cul-de-sac in Carson, California, right behind the Carson High School football field.

During that time, Mom was a foster parent to lots of kids. That meant there might be as many as six or seven foster kids living with us. It was like growing up in a preschool that had no other permanent students. For the longest time, I didn't have my own bed. I can remember being tired and asking Mom where I was sleeping that night. Sometimes it was two kids to a bed, but it didn't bother me. It was kind of fun and it was just the way life was. It all felt very normal.

When I was three years old, Burt Decker molested me. I'm not going to say any more about it, but it is part of who I am and it never goes away. When I was four, he moved out with one of the older foster kids, a sixteen-year-old girl. I never saw him again.

Over the next year, several other men came and went in our house, but only one stayed around long enough to make an impression. Mom told me that I should call him 'Dad.' Then they had a fight one night. She woke me up, told me to kiss him good-bye and that he wasn't my dad any more. I never saw him again. I was five when a man named Walt showed up. He stuck around. It wasn't long before he and Mom were married, and he really was my dad from then on.

For the most part, growing up in my mom's house was a happy experience. After all, she had picked me out of the never-ending river of foster kids and decided to keep me. I didn't know it at the time of course, but she had not led an easy life. She had married young to get out of a bad situation at home and went straight into a worse one with Burt Decker. He was controlling and violent toward her, although she managed to protect the kids from most of the bad stuff.

We never had a lot of money, but Mom was very creative about coming up with ways to have fun. I remember a birthday sleepover where she invited twelve girls over, which was way more than we had room for. Because my birthday is so close to Christmas, she assumed that most of them wouldn't be able to come. Fourteen girls showed up. She built a 'campfire' out of logs and Christmas lights. The next morning, we all piled into the van to go get donuts. Every time we came to a red light, Mom would yell "Chinese Fire Drill!" and we would all cascade out and run around the van like little maniacs, laughing and tumbling back into our seats when the light turned green.

There were a lot of kids my age in the neighborhood. We played Red Rover, Hide 'n Seek, Red Light, Green Light or baseball all day, and then had sleepovers at each other's houses at night. This being Southern California, the weather was always warm and I had a year-round tan. Disneyland and Knott's Berry Farm weren't far away, and Mom and Dad took me whenever they could. Then there were the beaches. My big brother Brian was a surfer, and I loved it when he would take me to the ocean with him and I could watch him surf. I was a California girl in every way.

Toward the end of sixth grade, Mom took me on a vacation to see my sister Shari, my niece Lori and my nephews Ed, Dane and Danny in Onalaska, Washington. We spent a week there and I went to school with Lori and her brothers. I loved her school. In Carson, there were a thousand kids in my grade. In Onalaska, there were only thirty. Mom seemed to like it too, because when we got back to California, she started talking about moving to Washington.

Mom was more about action than she was about talking, so she put the house up for sale and started packing. By the time someone bought the house though, I had already started school at Steven White Junior High. At first, I kind of liked the idea of moving, but then the cutest boy in the seventh grade started talking to me every day, and I didn't want to move any more.

My brother Brian was nine years older than me and had already enrolled in the police academy, so he told Mom and Dad that he was staying behind when we went. That meant that not only was I going to a place where I didn't know anyone and it rained all the time, I also wouldn't get to see my brother very often.

Before we moved, Dad took a trip to Washington to pick out our house in Onalaska. Mom decided to settle there so we could be close to Shari and Lori. All that summer, I lay out in the sun to get as tan as I could. By the time we were finally ready to move, I was as brown as I had ever been.

Mom and Dad drove to Washington in a U-Haul truck and Brian and I followed them in his van. The van had seats in the front and shag carpet in the back. I spent the trip either sleeping or annoying Brian, asking him a thousand questions. Brian influenced the way I thought about almost everything, but especially music. Whatever albums I had as a young girl—The Beatles, The Lovin' Spoonful, The Rascals—came as gifts from Brian.

I also liked to talk to him about his girlfriends. He was good-looking and a surfer, so he never had a hard time finding dates. I got attached to some of them, especially one girl named Meg. She was the perfect California girl—freckled, tan, and blonde. I felt like she was my sister. When things ended between Meg and Brian, I was much more heartbroken than he was. I spent much of the trip harassing him about why he broke up with her. I'm sure he appreciated advice on his love life from his baby sister.

Brian and I were always close, and I thought we always

would be. Instead, that trip was one of the last times I ever spent much time with him, and that left a hole in my life.

Even though we had planned to move to Onalaska, Dad hadn't been able to find anything he liked there in our price range. So instead of moving there, where I had already made friends at Lori's school, we were moving to another tiny town a few miles away called Mossyrock. Onalaska, Mossyrock…were there any towns with normal names in Washington?

When Brian and I turned off Highway 12 onto Damron Road, the first thing I noticed was how different it felt from home. The houses were a lot more spread out, with big gardens in most of the yards. A lot of the houses weren't houses at all, but single- and double-wide trailers. When we pulled into the driveway of a dilapidated red house with overgrown grass and a garage that looked like it would fall over in the next windstorm, Mom was standing in the front yard with her arms folded. She did not look happy. "This is the last time I ever send you ahead to pick out our house," she said to Dad. It was too late to do anything about it though. The papers had been signed and it was all ours, such as it was.

The house had three bedrooms and one bathroom. It was kind of rundown, but it sat on a big lot. That meant there would be lots of room for my two Dobermans, Peter and Chastity. Mom also promised me that we would have rabbits, and there might be room for a horse. I thought that was only fair. I figured that if I was going to live in the middle of nowhere, I should at least have a horse.

While I was exploring the house, Mom and Dad went outside to stand in the front yard. I had no idea what they were doing, but they had only been out there for a minute when I heard them talking to someone. I went out the front door and saw that Mom and Dad were talking to a stranger. He was old, or at least he looked old to my eleven-year-old eyes. He had dark hair, but there was a white streak in the middle, giving his hair the look of a skunk. He was smiling and friendly, listening to my mom. Behind him, a few feet away, I saw a tall, skinny teenager with a wrench working on a ten-speed bike. He had curly brown hair and black glasses. He seemed to be going out of his way to ignore everyone.

I had missed the beginning of what Mom was saying, but I

saw her waving up at the sky, telling a story with broad gestures. This was so embarrassing I thought I might die, so I went back in the house without bothering to find out anything else about our new neighbors.

Moving from Carson, California to Mossyrock, Washington was a huge adjustment. In California, there were hundreds of kids in my sixth-grade class. Starting seventh grade in Mossyrock, there were twenty-eight kids in my class. Twenty-eight! School had already started by the time we moved, so in addition to being the new girl, I got to be the new girl who arrived after everyone else had formed their groups.

Brian took me to school and helped me get registered that first day. I thought it would be a lot cooler if my surfer-dude brother took me to school instead of my Mom, who could usually be counted on to do something embarrassing. After we got all the paperwork filled out, Brian left and Mr. Alban, the principal, escorted me to meet the rest of my class.

The girls were in the high school gym doing P.E. because the boys were using the junior high gym. When we walked in, everyone stopped doing calisthenics and started playing 'check out the new girl.' They started talking, and one of them even pointed at me and laughed. I wished I was anywhere else but there. I regretted spending so much time working on my tan, because now I knew it just made me stand out that much more.

By the time I got there, P.E. was almost over, so I didn't have to dress down. Instead, I sat in the bleachers and tried to make myself small. When the bell rang, everyone changed back into their street clothes and walked in a group back to the junior high. I followed a few feet behind. One girl separated from the rest and started walking beside me.

"Hi. I'm Sheri. Where are you from?"

I guessed that she must be the leader of the pack. She was a cute girl with shortish blonde hair. She was dressed nice and looked friendly.

"Carson, California."

"Where's that?"

"Southern California, kind of by Los Angeles."

"What's your name?"

"Dawn."

She nodded. None of the rest of the girls were obvious about looking at me, but I still felt like a bug under a microscope.

"Really, there's just one thing you need to know. We don't like girls that steal our boyfriends."

I'd never had a boyfriend. I was so innocent I didn't really know what a boyfriend was.

I shrugged, nodded and mumbled something. I hadn't even met any of the boys in the junior high yet, and I sure didn't have any plans for a boyfriend.

"OK," Sheri said. "See ya 'round!"

I rode the #9 bus home that day, pretty happy with myself. I had met the popular girls and survived the experience. Most days when I got off the bus, my only chore was to do the dishes after dinner. So I watched whatever came on TV—*The Carol Burnett Show*, *Gilligan's Island*, *The Brady Bunch*—until Dad got home and switched over to watch the news. Then I would go in my room and watch my own little black and white TV, or listen to records and read my Archie comics. I always pulled for Betty to win Archie's heart, but he always seemed to go back to Veronica.

I fit in pretty well at my new school for the first week or so. One day, Mrs. Rhodes asked me to take a message over to the high school office. As soon as I walked through the double doors of the high school, I saw a group of high school boys gathered around their lockers. They were only freshmen, but I was a seventh-grader and they looked pretty old to me. I kept my head down and tried to walk by them, but a boy named Beau Pries stepped in front of me.

"Hey. You want to go to the Homecoming Dance with me?"

I froze a little inside, but managed to get out "Yeah, sure." The whole conversation lasted five seconds, but it seemed like I had a date to Homecoming.

I guess it's normal for older boys to always ask younger girls for dates, but in Mossyrock it was like the local pastime. I think the upperclassmen had asked out all the eligible freshmen girls, so the freshmen boys were reduced to looking for girls in the junior high. I was a little embarrassed, but also kind of excited. Beau was cute and popular, and a lot of the other girls liked him.

I dropped off the note at the office and hurried back to the junior high. I felt a little more excited with every step I took. I didn't think about needing a dress, or anything other than the fact that I was going to get to go to a high school dance.

When I got back to the junior high, it was between classes. I saw Sheri standing with a group of the other girls I had become friends with. I couldn't wait to tell her my news. "Guess what? Beau Pries asked me to Homecoming!"

I thought she'd be happy for me. Instead, her face clouded over and she burst into tears. She covered her mouth and ran down the hall away from me.

Uh-oh.

Brenda Whatley, who was also friends with Sheri, said, "Way to go. Beau and Sheri just broke up last week. She's been hoping they will get back together and go to Homecoming."

My brief time of peer acceptance in the halls of Mossyrock Junior High had just come to an end. I had broken the only rule I had been given: *Don't steal our boyfriends.*

Wouldn't It Be Nice

I felt like I'd been run over by a bus filled with crying teenage girls. One moment I was fitting in, making new friends, and loving my new school. The next, I had a date for Homecoming, but I was a social outcast. For the next week, I moved through school like I was invisible. My old friends disappeared, but no one new popped up to take their place. I knew we were in Washington to stay but I really missed California.

One day at lunch, another freshman boy, Chip Lutz, came down to the junior high and found me just as I stepped outside. Chip was tall, with dark hair and a great smile. Every time I saw him it seemed like he was joking around. Not today, though. Today he looked serious.

"Hey," Chip said.

"Hey."

"Listen. Things got kind of messed up with Beau asking you to Homecoming. He asked you out because he thought you were really cute and nice, but now he's getting crap from everyone."

"Is he? Gosh, I feel really terrible for him. That must be awful." Chip probably didn't get my sarcasm, but I had a hard time feeling sorry for Beau. He hadn't spoken a word to me since he asked me out, and now he was sending his friend to talk to me instead of having the guts to come himself.

"Yeah, well…" Chip seemed a little unsure how to continue. "Anyway, he thinks it would probably be better if you guys didn't go to Homecoming together."

"You know what? That works for me too. I think he's right."

I turned and walked to the multi-purpose room for lunch. I was surprised that I didn't feel that bad. I had been looking forward to the dance, but that was before I knew I had agreed to go with the wrong boy. It would have been so much easier if all the boys that were off-limits had to wear a sign around their neck. Then I would have known.

That afternoon when I got home from school, I was laying in my room listening to music when I heard a strange sound coming from outside. It sounded like a whoosh and a small explosion. When I pulled my curtains back a little bit, I saw the older boy from next door out in his yard. He was swinging a long bullwhip around his head again and again, cracking it very loudly. I thought about it for a minute, but I couldn't come up with any reason why he would do that. He was so tall and thin that he looked a little bit like a whip himself, so he looked kind of funny.

I slipped out our back door and wandered around outside where I knew he could see me. I thought he might be embarrassed, and might even stop cracking that silly whip. We both lived on half-acre lots, so he didn't have any cattle to herd or anything. He didn't seem embarrassed though. In fact, he ignored me completely, as older kids usually did with younger kids.

After about ten minutes of me trying to look like I was doing something, he spoke without looking at me.

"I can show you how to do this, you know."

"Not real sure I want to know how to do that, you know."

He shrugged, turned his back to me, and kept whirling the whip around his head, occasionally bringing it down to whip the head off a dandelion or weed poking through the ground. I was starting to think that was the end of our conversation and getting ready to go back inside, when he curled the whip up into small loops and sat down cross-legged on the grass. Now, he was looking at me.

"I'm Shawn."

"I know. I'm Dawn."

"Yeah, I know. So, we rhyme. Glad to get that out of the way. What do you like to do?"

"Nothin'. I mean, I don't know. Why? What do you like to do?"

He shrugged again. "I like to do lots of stuff. I like to read. Science fiction, mostly, and comic books. I like music. I like The Carpenters. I just got their album. Do you like them?"

"Um, no. I definitely do not like The Carpenters. They sound like the kind of music my parents listen to." I didn't tell him that I had kind of liked them when they were on The Muppet Show, because I thought that would be too uncool.

He nodded. He had this crazy, curly hair that went everywhere and seemed to live a life of its own. When he nodded, it bounced all over the place. We were sitting pretty close and I could see he had nice blue eyes, but they were kind of hidden behind his thick glasses.

"That's probably why. Because you're a kid. Maybe when you're a little older you'll like them."

I hated it when anyone talked down to me. "Nope. Don't think so. Crappy music is crappy music, no matter how old I am." I stood up, brushed the grass off my jeans and walked away. By the time I got to the front door, I could hear the whip cracking again.

I saw Shawn doing the strangest things out in the yard over the next few weeks. Sometimes he would be doing relatively normal things, like throwing a baseball or a football up in the air and catching it, but he also spent time using a badminton racquet to chase invisible things around the yard. Other times, he would stand in his driveway with a tiny little baseball bat and hit little rocks into the empty field across the street. Of all the boys in Mossyrock, I wondered why I got dropped down next to him.

In time, we started drifting together in the middle of the yard more and more often. Our conversations often started with him insulting me because I wasn't very tall, or because I was still young enough to go to the junior high. It wasn't unusual for them to end with him insulting me again, and me hitting him in the arm as hard as I could before I stormed away.

In between the insults and the fact that he couldn't ever seem to keep an opinion to himself, we became friends. Even though he was a teenage boy, he was kind and gentle. More importantly, he never seemed to judge me about anything, even though he teased me without mercy. I don't suppose that being kind and non-judgmental made a guy popular boyfriend bait in high school, but it made him perfectly qualified to be my friend. Ever since we had moved away from my brother Brian, I felt like something was missing in my life. Shawn stepped into that role naturally.

Eventually, the weather got colder and neither of us spent much time outside. That meant that we hung out a lot less, but he still came over to my house fairly often. He, Mom and I would sit around our living room and talk. Mostly, he and Mom would talk, and I would watch TV. When it was just Shawn and me hanging out, we talked about other kids and music and what shows were on that night. When Mom got added to the mix, they talked about his schoolwork or the presidential election, or other topics I never absorbed because I quit listening.

Shawn and Mom got to be friends too. I think she liked him because he was smart, but sometimes she didn't like him because he was a little too smart-alecky. One day in January, he dropped by the house and said he had something to ask us.

"So, I'm turning sixteen in a few weeks and my parents are throwing me a birthday party in town. I was wondering if you guys would like to come."

"Is this a teenager birthday party, or will there be adults there too," Mom asked.

"Mostly teenagers," Shawn said, "but my mom will be there too."

Shawn's mom being there was probably not a big selling point to my mom. She liked Shawn's dad, Robert, but she thought his mom, Ruth, was judgmental about everything and everyone. Once, Ruth sent Shawn over to borrow a can opener and Mom told him that I would run it over to her in a few minutes. She spent half an hour in the kitchen scrubbing that can opener so that it shined, because she didn't want his mom to think our house was dirty.

Still, she looked at me. I was silently pleading to go.

"OK, we'll be there, then."

When the day of the party arrived, I put on my best black slacks, white top and black jacket. It was as close to formal as it got in my closet. Right on time, Mom and Dad and I piled into the van and drove into town. The party was held in what passed for a community hall in Mossyrock. It wasn't fancy. In fact, it was just one big room with grey concrete floors and painted cinderblock walls.

I immediately regretted that we had gotten there on time, because hardly anyone else did. Mom and Dad sat down at a round table in the corner. It was just a little folding table, but Shawn's mom had covered it with a paper tablecloth and it looked nice. I went and got them some punch, then sat there nervously, waiting to see if anyone else I knew was going to show up.

Lots of kids soon started showing up, but they were all Shawn's age or a bit younger. I hardly knew anybody else there.

Shawn's mom made a show of unboxing the cake. The local cake lady had made it look just like the album cover for the new Wild Cherry album, the one with the lips and the cherry.

Once the music started, people started to dance. I sat at the table with Mom and Dad. It was pretty easy to notice that no one else had brought their parents to the party. I felt like I was five years old and too young to be allowed to cross the street on my own.

Soon, Shawn came over and asked me to dance. It was a fast song and as soon as the song faded out, I hurried and sat back down at the table again with Mom and Dad again. The idea of the party was kind of fun, but actually being there and not knowing anyone made me feel like I was what I'd been ever since I moved to Mossyrock—the new kid who doesn't know how to fit in.

The next few hours passed mercifully quickly. Shawn asked me to dance a few more times, but I knew why. He felt sorry for me because no one else was dancing with me. He was just being nice to the kid next door. Mom and Dad had been great to bring me to the party, and through the whole thing they sat there and watched without saying a word. I saw that they were fidgeting around a little bit, though, and I knew the party was almost over for me.

I think Shawn might have noticed we were getting ready to leave, because he came over and grabbed me and pulled me out on the floor for one last dance. Just as we got to the middle of the dance floor the song changed. Whatever fast song had been playing stopped in the middle, and after a few seconds *Stairway to Heaven* started to play. A slow song.

I'd been to a few dances at the junior high, sock hops after football games and that sort of thing, but this felt a little different. Those dances were with junior high boys. This was with a high schooler. I didn't want to chicken out, though, so I just kind of stood there, uncertain of what to do next.

Shawn casually walked up to me and pulled me gently against him, just like it was no big deal. We didn't really dance; it mostly amounted to shuffling our feet and moving in a circle. He was a lot taller than me, so it felt completely natural to put my arms up on his shoulders and lay my head against his chest. He was kind of sweaty, because he had been dancing a lot, but he smelled good.

When the song got a little faster, the couples around us moved apart and started dancing faster, but we stayed together. Shawn didn't grope me like the junior high boys always did during a slow song. Instead, he put his hand on the lower part of my back and moved it slowly and gently in a circle. No one had ever touched me like that before. It didn't feel racy or anything. Instead, it made me feel safe and warm.

As soon as the song ended, someone flipped on all the lights and I turned away from Shawn. I'm not sure why, but I felt embarrassed. When I got back to the table, I saw that Mom and Dad were already standing with their coats on. I grabbed my jacket and we were out the door before I had a chance to say goodbye to Shawn. I couldn't even remember if I had wished him a happy birthday.

On the car ride home, it felt like I could still feel the vibration that I felt while we were dancing to *Stairway to Heaven*. I didn't try to fool myself, though. I knew Shawn didn't like me that way. He was too old to be interested in me. He was more like my brother than anything else. Even so, it still felt warm where he had rubbed my back while we danced.

Thank You for Being a Friend

Mossyrock Junior High split each grade into two different groups. When I first moved there, I was put into the "A" group, but at the start of eighth grade, I got switched over to the "B" group. I had no idea why I had been in one group the first year and a different one this year. The inner workings of the Mossyrock Junior High faculty were a complete mystery to me. I had been ostracized by the girls in the "A" group since my near-date with Beau, so I didn't mind the switch at all. In the end, it turned out to be the best thing that could have happened. In the "B" group, I got to know Cheryl Hipps, Devy Ashe, Cindi Cowan and Missy Snodgrass. Maybe they weren't quite the popular girls who ruled the school, but they were real, honest, and nice. We all became best friends. We liked a lot of the same things, and none of them seemed overly concerned about whether or not I was trying to steal their boyfriends.

I was still so innocent that I didn't understand how things like dating worked. I was terribly shy, which didn't help either. A boy named Joe Woods asked me to go to a dance with him after a football game. I went, but we didn't say a word to each other the entire night. Another time, a boy I knew asked me if I would like to be Tim Johnson's girlfriend. I still didn't really get what that meant, because he never talked to me at school. Almost every night though, Tim would call me and we would talk on the phone. We never really broke up, but I figured it was over when he stopped calling me at night.

Going out with boys was just one more thing to do, like hanging out with my friends, riding horses, or watching TV. In those days, I never put much of myself into the whole dating

20

aspect of life. Having sleepovers with my friends and talking to them felt much more important.

I was nervous when it was time for me to start high school. I had gotten used to being one of the big kids in junior high, and we would all be starting from scratch in high school. One of the reasons I was a little wary was that I wasn't just the youngest kid in my class; I was the youngest by a lot. My mom had skipped me a grade when I was just starting school, so I was almost a full year younger than everyone else. Everyone else in my class was fourteen or fifteen already, but I wouldn't be fourteen until December 27th.

Also, I wasn't exactly the best student. When I was sitting in class listening to the teacher talking about algebra or European history, I had a hard time caring. Mom had been pretty tolerant about my grades when I was in junior high, but now that I was in high school, she said I had to do a lot better.

One day about a month after school started, I brought home a couple of bad homework grades and a bad test score. I thought about hiding them from Mom, but instead I decided to just get it over with. Sometimes it's a lot easier to take the hit and move on instead of dragging it all out.

"Here," I said, handing Mom the stack of papers. "I got some of my scores back."

Mom took them from me, peering over the tops of her glasses at me instead of looking at the homework.

"Am I going to be happy?"

"I think…. No, you probably aren't going to be happy."

She took a deep breath and held it, her steady gaze never leaving me. I tried to shrink a little bit, but there was no escaping that look.

She took her time, shuffling methodically through the papers. When she got through them all, she took another deep breath.

"Here's what we're going to do," she said. "You're going to go get Shawn from next door and bring him over here. I'm going to ask him to tutor you in…" she tilted her head back and looked through the bottom of her glasses at the papers, "Social Studies and Freshman English. I think he can handle those. And if he charges us for tutoring you, you can babysit and pay me back every penny of what I pay him."

"Aww, c'mon, Mom. I'll do better. I just…"

She interrupted me right there. "No, here's what you will 'just' do. You will 'just' march yourself over next door and ask Shawn if he will come see me." Her chin was raised and I knew I was beat. I sighed and walked out the front door, making sure not to close it too loudly. I tried to pick my battles and this one was already over.

I made my way next door, but I took my time. It was a nice day, or at least it had been until I had shown Mom my grades, so I went out back and checked on the rabbits in the hutch. They were all there, which was a relief. I liked raising rabbits. To me they were pets, but to Mom and Dad they were sometimes supper.

I walked out to the back pasture and watered my horse, Shilo. I petted his neck and talked to him for a few minutes. Eventually, I got the feeling I was being watched and looked over my shoulder at the house. Mom was standing in the kitchen window with her mouth a firm line and her eyebrows raised. I knew that look too, so I shrugged and made my way across the yard.

Shawn's parents always kept their yard and gardens perfect. They had huge Rhododendron bushes out front and little flower beds everywhere. It was just a double-wide trailer, but they always made it look nice.

I trudged up to the sliding glass door at the front of the house. I could see Shawn sitting inside, reading a comic book. I'm pretty sure he heard me come up the steps, but he kept reading the comic. When I knocked, he made a big show out of being surprised that I was standing there. He was a funny, funny boy, at least to himself.

"Hey," he said, opening the slider.

"Hey. Mom wants to know if you can come see her."

"Oh. Ummm…" He pretended to be thinking about it, like he was so busy he wasn't sure he could work us into his social calendar. Sometimes I just wanted to punch him. Sometimes I went ahead and did.

"OK," he said, smiling. At least he usually laughed at his own jokes, so I didn't have to.

We raced back across the yard and he beat me to my front steps. He tried to lean against the house like he had been waiting for me a long time, but I just gave him a quick kick on the way by and went inside.

"Hi," he said to my Mom, who was sitting in her chair looking very serious.

"Shawn, we have a situation and we need some help. Dawn is struggling a little bit with adjusting to high school and she's falling behind. We're worried that if she gets too far behind, she'll have a hard time catching up."

I swear to God, Shawn was standing in the middle of my living room frowning and holding his chin in his hand like a concerned grownup. Two minutes ago, he was joking and clowning around like a ten-year-old, and now this. I could've killed him.

"I know that you are in Honor Society and make good grades, so we're wondering if you would be willing to help us out and tutor Dawn one or two nights a week?"

Shawn nodded slightly, like he got asked to tutor people every day.

"Of course, we couldn't pay you very much," Mom added.

"Ah, that's OK. You guys have always been nice to me. I'm glad to help you out with this. Don't worry about it."

I was glad to hear him say that since it was going to come out of my babysitting money.

"Well, that's very generous. Thank you."

I never understood it, but somehow Mom always got people to do what she wanted, and usually for free.

Shawn got pretty sick after a few weeks, so we only had a few tutoring sessions, but they actually weren't all that horrible. Sometimes he came to my house after supper, and sometimes I went to his. We always sat at the kitchen table so we could spread my books out. Shawn had been like my big brother for a couple of years by then, but I started to feel closer to him while he was helping me with my studies. Sometimes he was kind of conceited and arrogant, but never when he was tutoring me. He never made me feel bad for not knowing something, even when he could have.

Since we were teenagers, we spent a lot of our study sessions talking about things other than History or English, especially when we were over at his house. At my house, Mom was always just a few feet away, listening to everything we said. At Shawn's house, his mom and dad never seemed to care.

One night, we talked about the upcoming Homecoming Dance, a Mossyrock fall tradition. A boy I was friends with, Gordon Brooks, had asked me to go, but I never even got a chance to tell Shawn. He seemed too excited about his own date.

"So," he said, "It's going to be so cool. I'm taking this girl from Seattle. Her name is Lorraine and she's a college girl! She goes to the UW. I met her at that Writer's Conference I went to last year. I never thought she'd actually go with me, but I asked her and she said she would."

I gave him a half smile that said, 'Oh, can't you see by my expression how excited I am for you,' but he was too slow to catch it. It wasn't that I expected him to ask me, and I already had a date, but it didn't make me happy that he was so excited about going with this other girl.

"It's gonna be great. She's going to come down and spend the night here…"

There was probably more to that sentence, but I had completely tuned him out by then.

"So what's the answer to question twelve?" I asked, interrupting him.

"Oh, ummm…." He looked at me a little oddly. I knew it was a breach of etiquette to interrupt our small talk with studying, but I thought that if he went on for ten more seconds about how much fun he was going to have with Lorraine, I might explode.

The situation got a little worse a few days later. Gordon had asked me to the dance as a friend, but we were walking along outside the high school when he leaned in and tried to kiss me. I turned my head. His lips met my forehead, which probably wasn't what he intended. It was awkward. The next thing I knew, Gordon was taking Lisa Hilton to the dance and I had no date for Homecoming. Again.

This was becoming a tradition I could live without. By then, we were only a few days away from the dance and I knew no one else was going to ask me, so I resigned myself to just staying home. On the day of the dance, I tried not to even think about all my friends getting their hair done, putting on makeup and dressing up for the dance, while I sat at home with Mom and Dad watching television.

There was a knock on our front door around 8:30. When I answered it, it was Shawn. He looked much better than when I first saw him two years ago. He'd gotten contact lenses earlier that year, and I could see his blue eyes much better. Sometimes, when we were sitting in the yard talking, he would be sitting so close to me that it felt like his eyes could see all the way through me. He had a new suit on that was a big improvement over the blue leisure suit he wore to other formal dances at school.

I thought about asking him where Lorraine was, but I was afraid he'd mistake that for a real question and answer me, so I didn't.

"Well, don't you look nice," Mom said when she saw him. Dad didn't bother to look away from the television.

"Oh, thanks," Shawn said. "You'll never guess what happened. Lorraine ended up having to go back to Moses Lake for a family emergency. So, I guess I'm going stag tonight."

My first instinct was to smile and say "Oh, that's too bad" in a completely insincere way, but instead I pretended to be so absorbed in *The Love Boat* that I was unaware of his existence.

Dad grunted and nodded a little, which I interpreted to mean, *Yeah, I kind of expected her to stand you up.* I put my hand over my mouth to hide my smile.

Mom just said, "Oh, I'm sorry…"

"It's alright," Shawn said with a sigh as he sat down on the couch beside me. "I'll survive."

We all watched *The Love Boat* for a few minutes—it was the episode where John Ritter dressed up like a woman to get on the cruise—and then Shawn stood up like he was going to leave.

"Say," Mom said, "Dawn was supposed to go the dance tonight too, but her date cancelled on her at the last minute too. We already had her dress ready though. Would you be willing to escort Dawn to the dance as a favor to us?"

Shawn looked a little surprised. *Hey! Going to the dance with me wouldn't be all bad, you know.* I kept that to myself, too.

"Um, sure, that'd be fine."

Mom looked at me. "Well, Sissy, go get your dress on. Don't keep him waiting all night."

I looked at Shawn. I wasn't sure he really wanted to take me, but he smiled at me and nodded. I jumped off the couch and ran into my room. I had taken a bath, but I hadn't done anything at all with my hair and I didn't have any makeup on at all. I didn't want to take the time for it, so I grabbed my dress off the hanger and threw it on the bed. I searched through my closet for the right shoes, but couldn't find them until I remembered they were at the edge of my bed. I had my clothes off and my dress and shoes on in about two minutes. I took an extra thirty seconds to run a brush through my hair, then hurried back to the living room.

When I walked in, Shawn was still standing and talking to Mom. He was in the middle of a sentence when I came in, but he stopped talking. He eyed me closely. I looked right back at him, raising my chin a little bit. I wondered why he was staring at me like that.

"Do I look OK?"

Shawn just nodded, Mom was smiling and for some reason, it looked like Dad was glaring at Shawn.

"Is this Dutch?" asked Mom.

Shawn did not grasp what she meant. "Um, I don't know. I'm not sure. I guess so."

I knew what Mom meant, but Shawn was oblivious. She stared at him like he might have gotten stupid all of a sudden. She sighed and turned to me.

"Go get me my purse then, so I can get you some money."

"Oh," Shawn said. "I thought you were asking if her dress was Dutch. No, no, no, I've got our tickets to get in and everything."

Mom looked pleased that he finally caught on. She gave me a kiss and told me to come home straight after the dance.

"We will," Shawn said. "I'm pretty sure it's over by midnight, but we'll leave by then even if it's not and I'll have her home."

It felt odd to be walking across the yard with Shawn. We had spent a lot of time together, but not with me in a dress and him in a suit and kind of going on a date.

Shawn drove a blue Vega. When we got to the car, he opened my door for me and made a sweeping motion with his hand and said, "Your carriage, m'lady."

"You're a dork."

He laughed, and it didn't really feel strange any more.

When we got to the dance we found a table and sat down. I was nervous about being around all the older kids, but Shawn stayed with me, and we talked and drank punch and laughed at the other couples. There was a live band and they were good, so we danced a lot. When they played *Desperado*, we slow-danced. He put his hand low on my back and moved it in a gentle circle, just like when we had danced to *Stairway to Heaven*. When the song ended and we sat down, I was thinking that I didn't want him to stop doing that.

The dance started to wrap up a little before midnight. I heard some of the other kids talking about a party somewhere and that there was going to be drinking, but Shawn took me straight home, just like he promised.

When we pulled into his driveway, he jumped out of the Vega and hurried around to open my door again. He made the same silly sweeping motion with his hand.

"Still a dork," I said.

He laid his hand against the back of my shoulder and we walked to my front door. I wondered if he was going to try and kiss me. I kind of wanted him to, but I was nervous about it too. He was prattling on about something, and of course he eventually insulted me, because that's what we did with each other. I took that opportunity to turn on my heel, go inside, and close the door behind me. It had been a great night.

Wonderful Tonight

Shawn bought his Vega with money he had made over the summer, so he didn't have to ride the #9 bus back and forth to school every day. That was great for him, but I was thirteen, and my choices were to take the bus or walk.

At first, it seemed to be an accident when he gave me a ride. I would be standing at the bus stop waiting, and he would pull out of his driveway and ask, "Wanna ride?" After a while, though, we both figured out we were doing it every day and I didn't even bother to go out to the bus stop any more. We would just meet at the Vega at 7:45 every morning. If I was a little late, he would start the car and listen to music while he waited for me. He was pretty nice, especially for an older guy.

One Monday morning in mid-October, though, Shawn wasn't there when I came out of the house. I waited for him until I heard the bus coming down Damron Road, then gave up and caught it. It was the same thing the next day and the next. After a week or so, I gave up on even going to the Vega and just went straight to the bus stop, but I had no idea where Shawn was. He could have been kidnapped by aliens or moved to Seattle to go to school for all I knew.

After a week of not knowing anything, I caught up to his friend Jerry in the hall. Jerry and Shawn had been best friends for a long time, but they were very different from each other. Shawn was tall and skinny with crazy curly hair. Jerry was shorter, but he was the cutest and most popular boy in school. Almost every girl I knew had some kind of crush on him.

Because we were both friends with Shawn, I didn't see Jerry that way, but I respected his opinion—probably too much. When I thought about trying out for cheerleader in junior high, Jerry told me not to because all the cheerleaders were snobby and he didn't think I was like that. As a result, I didn't try out. He also had a good fashion sense. Where Shawn seemed to wear whatever he had picked up off the floor of his bedroom that day, Jerry's outfits were always coordinated. He had become my own fashion adviser, but I never would have admitted it to him.

"Hi, Jerry. Do you have a second?"

"Well, hello," he said in a fake-suave voice. He was hardly ever serious.

"Do you know what's going on with Shawn? I haven't seen him all week."

"I went by and talked to his mom yesterday and she said he just had the flu. She said he's getting better. He should be back next week."

He wasn't back the next week, though, or the week after.

Finally, when I got home from school one day, Mom told me that she had talked to Ruth, Shawn's mom, and that Shawn had something called encephalitis. I'd never heard of it, but Mom said it was a problem with his brain, like maybe it was swelling up or something like that. Right after that, I heard that another girl in school, Linda Spencer, had the same thing, but no one seemed to know how they had caught it, or if they would get better, or what.

The picture we had taken at Homecoming came in, and they gave me both of our copies. I thought that was a good excuse to go next door and see for myself what was going on. I was pretty sure Mom wouldn't want me to go, so I didn't tell her.

When I knocked on the sliding glass door, Shawn's mom came around the corner from the kitchen, wiping her hands on a dishtowel. She looked tired and her face was pinched in a knot of worry.

"Hello, Dawn."

"Hi. Ummm... the pictures I had taken with Shawn at the Homecoming Dance came in today, so I wanted to bring his over to him."

"That's very nice of you."

She reached out and took them from me and slid the pictures out of the little white envelope. She smiled a little. "That's a good picture. You looked beautiful."

"Thanks. Well, I guess I'll go home..."

"Do you want to go back and see Shawn?"

That surprised me. I hadn't thought about actually seeing him. I didn't really understand what he had, and I didn't know if he was contagious or not. I was pretty sure Shawn's mom wouldn't have invited me to see him if I could catch something, though.

Shawn's room wasn't actually part of the mobile home. It was a room that his dad had attached to the side of the trailer. We walked to the back of the house and stepped down into his room.

It was dark inside. The only light came from his black and white television, which was tuned to the afternoon movie with the sound turned almost all the way off. It felt stuffy, like the air had been recirculated too many times. Shawn's twin bed was in the corner and I could barely see him as he lay there.

"Shawn," his mom said. "Dawn's here. She brought you something." Her voice sounded very loud in the near-silent room. "You probably don't want to stay long, I know. If you talk to him for a few minutes, he might wake up for you or he might not. He's sleeping almost all day now."

I nodded and felt my throat get a little thick. When we were outside, or hanging out together, or studying, Shawn was always energetic. Now he just laid there.

"Uh, hey…" My voice sounded tiny and hollow. I didn't like the way it sounded. "So, we got our pictures back from Homecoming. I think they turned out pretty good." I was feeling a little foolish, like I was talking to myself. "Not much going on at school. It's school…"

He stirred and groaned a little, then tried to push himself up on his elbows. He squinted at me like the almost-total darkness wasn't dark enough. "Oh. Hi." His voice was weak and he sounded completely out of it.

"Hi. I didn't think you were going to wake up. I brought you your copy of the Homecoming picture we had taken." I took the little cardboard frame and set it on the table beside his bed. He acted like he hadn't heard me.

"Who are all those people with you?"

That threw me for a loop. I looked over my shoulder and then back at him.

"What do you mean? I'm alone. There's nobody here but you and me."

He nodded like he understood, but immediately lay back

down and closed his eyes. I waited for another minute to see if he was going to say anything else, but eventually I gave up and left. I felt worse than before I went to see him. He looked so bad I wondered if he would ever get up.

When I got home, Mom could tell I was upset and asked me where I had been. When I told her, she yelled at me and asked me if I wanted to catch whatever Shawn had. I didn't catch anything, though, and he eventually got better, but he didn't come back to school until just a few weeks before Christmas break. I was so happy to see him that first day, sitting in the Vega defrosting the windows. Not just because it was nicer getting a ride to school, but because I had missed him. I was pretty sure he just thought of me like his kid sister, but sometimes when he looked at me with such a serious look in his eyes, I thought maybe there was something more there.

Just before Christmas break, Shawn, Jerry and their friends Bill Woods and Chip Lutz did the weirdest thing. The year before, they had performed at the Mossyrock Talent Show by imitating KISS, the band with the makeup and platform shoes and loud music. They hadn't won a prize that night, but the crowd liked them and I could tell they had fun playing dress-up. The really weird thing was, none of them could really sing or play an instrument, so they just played a KISS song on a stereo, and pretended to play and sing along.

I told you it was weird.

I thought after the Talent Show that would be the last of it, but as soon as they were all back in school, they started planning an entire show where they would play KISS albums and pretend to play and sing. On the one hand, I thought they were crazy. Who would show up to see them do that? On the other hand, it was Shawn and Jerry, and they seemed to accomplish most anything they set out to do.

Their show was scheduled to be held in the multi-purpose room in the high school the night after school let out for Christmas vacation. I can't remember how much they were charging for tickets, but it wasn't very much. So Cheryl, Devy, Missy and I all decided to go. It might have been lame, but it was December in Mossyrock and there wasn't anything else going on.

On the night of the show, I was sitting on the couch in the living room when I heard something coming up the front steps.

When I opened the door, all I saw was this huge black figure looming over me, wearing horrible black and white makeup. It looked like a seven-foot-tall bat come to roost on our front porch.

I screamed. Loud. Like a horror movie scream. Mom jumped up out of her chair and took two steps toward the front door when the creature burst through the door laughing.

It was Shawn, dressed up in his Gene Simmons costume, makeup and platform shoes. He was laughing so hard, I was afraid he was going to hurt himself. I punched him as hard as I could, which wasn't very hard, because I was still getting over being scared. Mom looked at him in his ridiculous get-up and then at the expression on my face before bursting out laughing too. It's no fun being the only mad person in a room full of people who are laughing at you, so I had to give up being mad, at least on the inside.

Of course, Shawn had just wanted to come over and show us his costume before the show. Being Shawn, he had taken advantage of a great opportunity to scare me. Seen in the light of my living room, he wasn't all that scary, but he sure had been climbing up our front steps like a demented spider.

My friends and I went to the show, and it was all right. Someone had forgotten to turn the heat on and there were no chairs, so we all stood around in the multi-purpose room in our coats trying to stay warm. My musical tastes ran more to Three Dog Night and The Beach Boys than KISS, so I didn't really love the music. It was fun to see my friends up there on stage, jumping around in their costumes and tall platform shoes. We kept waiting for one of them to fall off their shoes, but they never did.

Much later, Shawn told me that he and Jerry had started imitating KISS because they thought it would be a good way to meet and impress girls. If he had wanted to impress this girl, he would have done a lot better impersonating Leif Garrett instead of Gene Simmons, but I never told him that.

After that, there were about ten days of Christmas vacation left. Our family didn't have a lot of money, so Christmas was never about getting a lot of new clothes or records or electronics or anything. That Christmas, my present was a pink princess phone that I could plug into an outlet in my room; pretty much the best present ever.

We always celebrated Christmas on Christmas Eve. We all

got dressed up like we were going out somewhere special, and Mom made us a huge Christmas dinner with a turkey and mashed potatoes, homemade bread with apple butter, glorified rice and Jell-O salad made with pineapple and cottage cheese. We didn't normally say grace, but we always did on Christmas. After dinner, we watched TV while Mom crocheted until Dad went to bed. On a normal night I would go to my room too, but on Christmas Eve Mom and I always stayed up really late and watched some old movie on Channel 13. That year we watched *The Hound of the Baskervilles*, which she was really excited about. I can't say I was, but it was fun staying up with the whole house quiet and just the two of us.

My birthday was two days after Christmas. When I was a little kid, Mom had made a big deal out of my birthday, but that had stopped as I got older. Mom made me a German chocolate cake, my favorite. They gave me a pretty necklace and some gloves, and I thought that was the end of the excitement for the day.

Just before lunch though, Shawn called. That was a little unusual because he and his family had gone to see his sister up near Seattle for Christmas and they hadn't gotten home yet. Long distance was expensive, so I was surprised to hear from him.

When the phone rang, I answered it.

"Dawn? Hey. Happy Birthday. Today is your birthday, isn't it?"

"Yep."

"Well, I'm up in Auburn at my sister's house right now, but I'm gonna leave to come home in just a little while. Anyway, I heard that *Star Wars* is playing out town so I think I'm going to go tonight. Since it's your birthday and I didn't get you anything else, I thought maybe you'd like to go with me?" ('Out town' was Mossyrock slang for going to Centralia or Chehalis, which were not large towns but had much more to offer a teenager than Mossyrock.)

My entire plans for the evening had been to have dinner with Mom and Dad and watch TV for a few hours, so going out town to see *Star Wars* sounded awesome. Mossyrock had a small movie theater called The G Theater, but the theaters out town were much nicer.

"Yeah, I guess. Hang on, I'll ask Mom if I can go."

I turned to Mom with a pleading look on my face. "Shawn wants to take me to a movie out town for my birthday. Can I go?"

She didn't even hesitate. "Sure."

I felt excited and happy, but I casually said "OK, I can go."

"Great! I'll pick you up at 5:30."

Mom made me homemade enchiladas for my birthday. We had a piece of my cake for dessert after dinner, and were done by 5:00. I went to my room and changed into my best slacks and top, and put my makeup on. I wanted to be a little more prepared for this date than I was for Homecoming.

Shawn got there a few minutes early and sat in the living room, where he talked with Mom and Dad about the weather and other boring stuff. He finally looked over at me and I gave him a look: *I thought we were going to the movies*. He smiled and stood up, ready to go.

"Which theater are you taking Dawn to?" Mom asked.

"The Fox in Centralia."

"And what are you going to see?"

"*Star Wars.*"

I could see that this meant nothing to Mom, but she didn't seem to care.

"What time does the movie play?"

"7:05."

"And what time will you have her home?"

"We'll come straight back and we should be here right around 10:00."

I was starting to get a little embarrassed by the interrogation, but I knew that if I objected, Mom was likely to make it worse and start asking if the tread on the tires on the Vega was okay, so I just squirmed silently.

"OK, you can go. We'll be waiting up."

We were out the door, running across the yard together in seconds. This time, I beat him to my side of the car and opened the door for myself. As soon as we got inside, Shawn started the car, turned the heater on full blast, and turned up the radio. It was just like every morning when he picked me up for school, except we were going out town.

I didn't really think this was a date, even though we were in his car and going to a movie. When he asked me, he made it seem like he was going anyway and invited me along so he didn't have to go alone. Plus, even though I was fourteen now, he was seventeen and a senior.

Usually when we were in the car, Shawn wouldn't shut up and I couldn't get a word in, but tonight he was quiet for a long time. We listened to the radio and I watched the nighttime scenery whiz past. After about twenty minutes, *Tonight's the Night by* Rod Stewart came on the radio.

"You know what I heard?"

I looked at him, but didn't say anything. When Shawn started sentences with 'You know what I heard?' what came next was often silly and ridiculous.

"I heard Rod Stewart had to go to the emergency room and get his stomach pumped because he had too much semen in it." He nodded enthusiastically after dropping that bombshell, as if that would confirm that it was true. I looked at him, waiting to see if there was more, but that seemed to be the sum total of his wisdom concerning Rod Stewart.

"You know what I heard? I heard you're an idiot."

I liked Rod Stewart and thought he was kind of cute for an old guy. I thought that boys knew that girls thought he was cute and that was why they made up stupid stories like that about him. I didn't really know how to put that into words though, so I just narrowed my eyes at him, shook my head, and looked forward. Shawn didn't say anything for quite a while after that, and I didn't have any real conversation starters either, so we rode the rest of the way to the theater without talking. When we pulled up in front of The Fox Theater, it was still completely dark inside. It did say "*Star Wars* 7:05" on the marquee, but it was only a little after 6:00.

Shawn smiled and said, "I got us here early so we could drive around town and look at everyone's Christmas lights. I just wanted to come by the theater and double-check that the show really started at 7:05, so we wouldn't be late."

He put the Vega back into gear and drove us all around Centralia. Two days after Christmas, everyone still had their lights up and it was pretty. Eventually he pulled into a 7-11.

"I just need to pick up something real quick, then we can go. You want to go in?"

I opened my door and got out. We had three little grocery stores in Mossyrock, but none of them had very big candy selections. The 7-11 felt like it was all candy and snacks. I was still full of chocolate cake and enchiladas, so I didn't want any, but it was kind of fun to just stand and look at everything.

Eventually, I saw Shawn pick up a pack of Freshen-Up gum. I had heard some of the girls at school talking about Freshen-Up, so I said, "Do you know what we call that kind of gum?"

He looked uncertain, but shook his head a little.

I leaned up and whispered in his ear. "We call it cum gum."

Shawn's eyebrows went up in surprise and he laughed. He also looked a little embarrassed.

When we got back to the Fox, there were lights on and a few people moving around, but we were still able to find a parking spot right in front of the theater. Shawn bought our tickets and we went inside, but I was starting to get a little worried. I had needed to go to the bathroom for the last hour and I knew I would never make it through the whole movie, but I didn't want to tell Shawn that I had to go.

"Do you want anything from the snack bar?" Shawn asked. "I'm gonna get some Hot Tamales."

I told him I didn't want anything but that I needed to go wash my hands before we sat down. It was months before I could actually tell him I needed to go to the bathroom. I don't know if he ever figured out that 'I need to wash my hands' meant the same thing.

When I came out of the bathroom feeling a lot better, Shawn was waiting for me with a smile. He reached out and laid his hand on my shoulder, then nodded toward the staircase that led up to the balcony. We found a seat right in the front row, so we looked right down on the screen. Eventually, the theater got pretty crowded, but it felt very comfy hanging out there like it was just the two of us.

Star Wars was good. I know some people think it is the greatest movie ever. I wouldn't go that far, but I liked it. I thought Luke Skywalker was cute. Looking back, I'm not sure what I saw there. When the movie was over, Shawn checked his watch. We just had time to get home by my curfew. The ride back went by fast. It felt like we had just left the theater when we were pulling into his yard. My birthday started out kind of plain, but it had turned out pretty great.

I didn't know if Shawn would walk me to my door again,

like he had when we had gone to Homecoming, or if he would just say goodbye and go into his house. It didn't matter either way, so I just got out and headed for my front door. I was at the front of the car when Shawn jumped out and stopped me. It was really cold outside, but Shawn looked so serious that I didn't even notice it. He stared at me so intently that I wanted to say 'What?' but I didn't. I just stared at him. He smiled a tiny smile but didn't say anything; he just kept looking at me. Finally, he gently took hold of my shoulders and pulled me close to him. He put his hands on my face and bent his head down and kissed me, soft and slow.

It wasn't my first kiss...but it was my first kiss like *that*. My knees felt like they were going to buckle on me, and electricity ran through my whole body. Every thought I ever had vanished from my head.

Shawn smiled at me again. He looked so happy. I felt happy too, but I really couldn't speak. We backed away and never took our eyes off each other. Finally, I turned away and walked to my front door. When I opened the door, Mom was there, still sitting in her chair, waiting.

"How was the movie?"

"Fine."

"Well, did you have fun?"

"Uh-huh."

"Uh-huh? That's it? Really?"

"Uh-huh. I'm tired. I'm going to bed."

She smiled at me. "That's fine, Sissy. Go to bed. I'm glad you had a good birthday."

I walked into my bedroom and turned off the light. I kicked my boots off and fell across the bed, hugging my pillow tight against my chest. After a minute I changed into my jammers, turned the light back off, and climbed into bed. I didn't think about anything but Shawn, and what it felt like when he kissed me.

Love is in the Air

I had decided that nothing was ever really going to happen between Shawn and me. Two years ago, we had danced at his birthday party, which had felt very nice, but I was too young for anything else. This fall we had gone to Homecoming together, but he got sick right after that and everything fizzled. Then he called me out of nowhere on my birthday and took me to see *Star Wars,* but absolutely nothing happened between us again after that.

I did my best to forget about him and spent time with my friends instead. I still had my friends Cheryl, Devy, and Missy, but I had also finally become friends with the girls I had gotten crosswise with when I first got to Mossyrock. We went to each other's houses after school and on the weekends, and had lots of sleepovers.

When Spring Vacation came at the end of March, I didn't have a lot planned. Shawn was going on a trip over Spring Vacation. He had made a pretty big deal about having a car and being able to go "somewhere," without really knowing where he was going. Whatever.

Before he left on his trip, Mom gave him a little surprise. When he had brought the Vega home the summer before, Mom had come out to look at it. It was a nice car. It was a pretty blue color and the interior was all done in blue and white. It had a hatchback, so when the back seat was folded down, it looked like a little bed. As soon as Mom saw that, she said it was like a little sin bin. Shawn liked that so much, he started calling it "The Sin Bin."

While he was loading it up with his sleeping bag and backpack for his trip, Mom walked out and handed him two pillows she had made that said "sin" and "bin." She thought she was funny, and Shawn seemed to really like them. I didn't know if he was having other girls in the back seat of the car or not, but I didn't like to think about it.

In the middle of our Spring Break week, I was invited to a sleepover at Devy's house. Missy, Cheryl, Cindi, and Carolyn were all going to be there. Our sleepovers weren't exactly epic, but they were fun. Mostly we hung out in the bedroom, listened to records and talked about boys; who was cute, who we liked, that sort of thing. The day of the sleepover, Mom went out to the street to check the mail like she did almost every day. She came back in with a fistful of bills and a circular from the grocery store in Morton, and said, "Oh, you got a letter from Shawn."

That was really weird. I had a pen pal in New Zealand who sent me letters, but I couldn't imagine a single reason why Shawn would send me something when he could usually just walk across the yard and tell me.

Standing in the middle of the living room, I opened the envelope. There was a single piece of notebook paper, with writing on just one side:

Dear Dawn,

I'm sure you're surprised to get a letter from me while I'm gone, but there are some things I want to tell you. We've been friends for a long time now, and I've always been more of a big brother to you than anything else. Lately I've been having feelings toward you that aren't "brotherly."

As I was sitting here I realized something and I want to say it right out loud. I love you. I suppose I started to love you quite a while ago, but it wasn't until right now that I realized it completely. I know it's strange telling you this in a letter, but I couldn't stand another day going by without telling you how I feel.

I don't have any idea if you feel anything other than friendship toward me. If you don't that's fine. Just throw this letter away and I'll never mention it again. I'll be home in a few days and if you want to, we can talk about it then.

Shawn

I looked up and saw Mom was squinting at me over the top of her glasses. Mom read every piece of mail I ever got, so I didn't even try to hide it. I handed her the letter and sat down in Dad's chair beside her. My head was spinning a little. While she read the letter, I tried to make sense of it.

Shawn loves me? Why did he wait until he was so far away before he told me? Why hadn't he just told me while we were sitting in the yard or driving to school?

Do I love him? That idea was a little bigger than I was ready to process right then. I had loved him like my brother for a long time, but he was talking about a different kind of love. My feelings for him had grown and changed over the last two and a half years, but I wasn't sure what that kind of love felt like.

But then, all that faded away... *Shawn loves me. Shawn loves me. Shawn loves me!*

Maybe I didn't really know what that kind of love was yet, but I thought about all the time we had spent together, talking and teasing each other, the way his eyes always seemed to change when he looked at me and how gentle he was when he touched me. And that kiss. That kiss.

Mom cleared her throat to bring me back to the living room. Her head was cocked slightly to the right and a tiny smile played across her lips.

"He said he wanted to tell you he loved you 'right out loud.' By writing it in a letter. I'm not too sure about that kid."

I shrugged my shoulders but didn't say anything. I took the letter from her and tucked it back into the envelope. "I'm gonna go listen to music in my room."

She nodded and smiled at me like she understood.

I closed the door to my bedroom and went over to my little record player. It was the kind that had a lid and a handle so I could carry it around if I wanted. I had the 45 of *If* by Bread. I dropped it on the spindle, set it to repeat, and lay down on my bed.

I'd thought Shawn was too much older to be interested in me. Now he said he loved me. I'd never let myself think about the feelings I knew had been growing for him, because it never felt like there could be a chance for there to be an 'us.' Now it felt safe to open my heart, at least a little, and feel what I had been hiding from everyone, including myself. I never felt safe opening up that part of me with anyone else, but it was different with Shawn. I didn't even have to think about it. I knew I trusted him.

That afternoon, I brought Shawn's letter with me to the sleepover at Devy's house. As soon as we settled in and started talking, I brought it out and showed it to Cheryl and everyone. It made me feel good that someone—especially Shawn—loved me, and I wanted to share it with my friends. Besides, at every sleepover the talk always turned to boys, and I had talked about Shawn quite a bit.

The letter was a hot topic of conversation for a few minutes. Everyone was happy for me. I started to think that maybe I hadn't hidden my feelings about Shawn as well as I thought. Either way, the talk moved on to other boys, so I slipped the letter back into my bag. I couldn't forget about it, though, and after everyone else had fallen asleep, I took it out and read it over again and again.

I thought that when Dad had brought me home from Devy's house that I might see Shawn's Vega parked in the driveway, but it wasn't there. The rest of the day dragged by. Every time I looked out my window, his parking spot was still empty.

When I woke up the next morning, I peeked out my window and there it was. The Sin Bin had returned. I wondered where he had gone and what he had seen. I wondered how he would act, now that he had sent me the letter.

I got dressed and went outside and walked around the yard, but Shawn was nowhere in sight. I saw his mom out on their patio and waved to her, but that was all. Finally, I heard music coming through our screen door. When I looked out, I saw that Shawn had both doors and the hatchback open on the Vega. I burst through the screen door and ran to him, but before I got there I stopped and walked the last few steps. It was a nice day and the car was already warm, so I leaned against the side of the car and looked up at the sun.

Shawn poked his head outside and looked at me for a long time. I looked right back at him and thought how much I had come to like his face. It went perfectly with the rest of him.

"Hey," he said.

"Hey."

Pretty exciting. Send me a letter telling me you love me, then when you see me you just say "Hey?"'

"Um, I'm going up to Auburn today to see my sister Terri and her son Tommy. Do you want to come?"

Inside, I thought that a day of driving around with Shawn

and going to a city that wasn't Mossyrock sounded great. Outside, I shrugged and said, "I guess. I'll have to check with Mom and see if I can go."

I turned and walked back to the house. A smile overtook me. Mom was just finishing the lunch dishes when I walked in the kitchen.

"Shawn wants me to go to Auburn with him. He's going to see his sister."

"Do you want to go?"

I nodded.

She shrugged and said, "That's fine, Sissy, but don't be out late."

"We won't."

"When are you leaving?"

"I...don't know. Hang on." I ran to the front door and pushed the screen door open. "When are we leaving?"

He gathered up a bag of garbage he'd taken out of the Vega and stared at me for a second, smiling. "Right now. Let's go!"

I poked my head back inside and said, "We're leaving right now. Bye. I love you," and thirty seconds later I was headed down Damron Road in the Vega. Things always seemed to take forever or happen very fast with Shawn. There was nothing in between. I didn't really know how far away Auburn was, but I knew it was farther than Centralia or Chehalis, so I settled in to enjoy the ride. It was a perfect sunshiny day, so we rode along with the windows rolled down, blowing our hair around. Shawn had the radio on, first listening to KITI in Centralia and then switching around the Seattle radio stations.

When we had driven about an hour, we passed through Olympia. Shawn pointed to a restaurant that sat beside the freeway.

"That's the Falls Terrace. I've heard it's a great place to eat."

I looked at the restaurant and thought it looked fancy and expensive. My experience with fancy and expensive restaurants was zero, so I just nodded.

"You know what? I think we should eat there sometime."

I turned in my seat to look at him. We had never even eaten at the A&W in Mossyrock, and now he wanted to take me to someplace an hour away from home that looked like it cost more money than either of us had?

"OK, sure. We can go eat there sometime."

"Great. How about April 29th?"

It was March 30th, so that seemed like a lot of pre-planning for a date we were never likely to take anyway.

"So now 'sometime' is April 29th, huh? Alright, we can go to dinner on April 29th."

"It's a date, then. Remember that date. April 29th."

I looked at him suspiciously, like maybe he was also going to ask me to fly to the moon with him, because that was about as likely as us driving to Olympia for dinner on April 29th. He smiled his innocent smile that he knew let him get away with almost anything and started singing along with the song on the radio.

Here's the thing. Shawn loved to sing all the time, but especially to songs on the radio. He didn't sing very well and he knew it, but he kept singing anyway. It made him happy. The fact that he sang around me made me feel like he trusted me, and that made me happy.

After another half hour or so, we got off the freeway and started driving through what I assumed was Auburn. I didn't know how big Auburn was, but it was a lot bigger than Mossyrock. It felt like we had driven around town for a long time, and I was beginning to wonder whether we were ever going to get to his sister's house. We were sitting at a red light when he reached down and turned the radio way up.

"Do you like this song?"

It took me a few seconds to recognize it, but then I remembered that it was *Always and Forever* by Heatwave.

"Mm-hm."

"I do too. Hey, did you know this is going to be the theme of the Prom?"

I didn't, but things were starting to fall into place.

"Yep, it is. And, did you know that Prom is going to be on April 29th?" Then, he snapped his fingers and acted like he had just made a connection himself. This was one of his favorite tactics. "Hey. Since we're already going out to dinner that night…"

I felt a little thrill of happiness run all through me.

"Are you asking me to Prom?"

"Yeah. What do you think?

I just looked at him. I felt so happy and he looked so nervous that it made him even cuter.

"Well, will you go with me?"

"Of course!"

I almost always hid my emotions, but this time I just couldn't. I threw my arms around his neck and buried my face in his chest for a moment. When I looked up at him, he had the biggest, goofiest grin on his face. If I'd looked in the mirror, I think I might have seen the same expression on my face. In so many ways, it felt like we had been building to this moment ever since we had become friends.

An obvious question might be why Shawn asking me to Prom had more impact on me than writing a letter telling me he loved me. The letter came from far away and didn't seem real. This—sitting in the warm sunshine in the Vega, feeling him beside me while he asked me to Prom in his own silly, frustrating way—felt completely real. I just wanted to sit there and soak it up, which we did until the light turned green and the people behind us honked their horn. Then we drove on to his sister's house, which wasn't much farther at all. It was a nice place on a hill above the city. It had a pool that I would have loved to go swimming in.

When we got out of the car and walked into the house, Shawn reached down and took my hand in his. It was the first time we had ever held hands, and it felt completely right.

He just walked right in without ringing the doorbell. His nephew Tommy was standing in the kitchen, looking surprised to see us. I thought Shawn had called ahead and that they knew we were coming, but apparently he hadn't. Even though Tommy was his nephew, he was almost the same age as Shawn, just like my niece Lori and me.

"Hey, PSI. What are you doing up here?" I knew that Shawn's first name was Patrick, but I had never heard anyone call him that before. I was learning all kinds of new things today.

Shawn shrugged, smiled, and looked a little guilty. "Oh, you know. Just came up to see what you guys are doing. How's TL?"

I figured that was Terri, his sister. *Maybe they're big on initials in their family.*

"She stayed home sick from work today, but I think she was more sick of going to work than actually sick. She's upstairs, c'mon."

Without asking me if I wanted to go into his sister's bedroom when she was sick, Shawn started walking down the hall and up the steps. Since we were still holding hands, I went too. When we walked into her bedroom, Terri actually didn't look sick at all, but she did look beautiful. She was sitting up in a king-sized bed, wearing a green nightgown. She looked at Shawn and glanced at our hands knitted together. She looked at me and smiled broadly.

"Well, hello," she said, like we had been friends forever but just hadn't met yet. "So you're Dawn. Shawn has told me so much about you."

He has? I looked at Shawn, but he was looking out the window like he wasn't paying attention to our conversation.

"Come here, sit down and talk to me."

I felt really funny even being in her bedroom, and now she wanted me to sit on her bed. I let go of Shawn's hand and kind of half-stood/half-leaned against the bed. She pretended not to notice I hadn't sat down.

"So, Dawn, what are you doing hanging out with these two yahoos? You look like a young lady of much greater taste and discernment than that."

I smiled but didn't answer, because I really wasn't sure what she had just said.

She looked over at Shawn and said, "So, PSI, are you getting ready to go to Alaska?"

I'm sure I looked a little surprised, because this was the first I had heard about this. The first summer after I moved to Washington, Shawn had spent the summer in Alaska with his brother Mick, but I didn't know he was planning to go back.

"Psssh. No. Not yet. That's almost two months away. I won't get ready to go until about ten minutes before I have to go to the airport."

So he was going to Alaska. I wondered why that had never come up in our conversations. If I was planning a big trip, I'm pretty sure I would have mentioned it to him. I felt my heart fall a little bit. We were just getting started. I didn't want him to go away already.

"Have you ever been to Laserium?" Tommy asked. I realized he was looking at me.

Again, I had no idea what that was, so I shook my head.

"It's at the Pacific Science Center, right next to the Space Needle. They play cool music and flash laser beams all over the ceiling. Do you want to go?"

"Yeah, sure, but what time does it happen?"

I was thinking that if we had to drive to Seattle, see the laser show, drive back to Auburn, and then back to Mossyrock, we'd be late getting home.

He ran downstairs, got the phone book, and called the information line for Laserium. The first show for the day was at 5:00.

"Why don't you call your mom and find out if it's alright?" Shawn asked. He pushed the phone at me.

I was a little embarrassed to talk on the phone with everyone standing around looking at me, but I dialed our number. Mom answered.

"Mom? It's Dawn."

"I know that. I recognize your voice. Are you OK?"

"Yes, sure, we're fine. Shawn and Tommy want to go into Seattle and go to a show at the Laserium, but if we go to that, we'll be home kind of late—probably around 9:30 or so. Is that OK?"

I heard a few seconds of silence on the other end of the line.

"No, honey, that's too late. Why don't you save that for the next time you go visit?"

"Oh. OK. Bye."

I was disappointed, but not because we weren't going to go see Laserium. I hadn't even known that existed until two minutes ago. I was the wet blanket that made it so Tommy and Shawn couldn't go, even if it wasn't my fault. They read the disappointment on my face.

"Don't worry about it," Tommy said. "Let's just go down to SeaTac Mall and see a movie. I have no idea what's playing, but they've got six theaters, so there's got to be something good, right?"

If there was something good, we didn't choose it. We ended up seeing a movie called *The One and Only*, starring Henry Winkler. It was terrible and it didn't matter. We had fun hanging out.

After we bought our tickets, we were waiting in line to get some popcorn when Tommy saw a pretty girl in the lobby. I think he wanted to impress us with how smooth he was, so he started talking to her. It did not go well.

"Let's make like Paul Simon and slip-slide away from this disaster," Shawn said. He took my hand and led me down the hallway to the theater where our movie was playing, leaving Tommy all alone. Tommy found us a couple of minutes later.

"Thanks for leaving me dying out there."

"You were dying with or without us," Shawn said. "So we thought we would limit your embarrassment by leaving you to it."

We watched the movie in silence but held hands through most of it. About halfway through the movie, I felt so close to Shawn that I rested my head on his shoulder and stayed that way until the credits rolled.

We got out of the movie just in time to drop Tommy back off at his house and head home. I was feeling so tired I thought I might fall asleep on the drive. About halfway home though, I saw a little orange car keeping pace with us in the fast lane. When I peeked around Shawn at the driver, I saw that he was holding a badge against his window and he was motioning us to pull over.

"Shawn, there's a guy in that car that wants us to pull over."

"Oh, really? I hadn't noticed."

He didn't look over at the cop though. He stepped on the accelerator instead, so I think he had already seen him. I don't know why, but I started to laugh. Shawn arched his eyebrows at me like I might be crazy, but he didn't slow down. The faster he drove, the harder it made me laugh. Shawn swerved the Vega at the very last minute as we were almost past an exit ramp, and we skittered a little bit before slowing down. The cop's car kept heading on down the freeway. Shawn pulled over onto the shoulder and I could see his hands were shaking a little bit, which made me laugh even harder. Finally, he looked at me and started to laugh. We sat there for a few minutes before pulling back onto the freeway, and made our way safely home.

We got home before my curfew, and Shawn walked me home. I was so tired I wanted to lie down and go to sleep right on the front lawn. It had been a big day. When it started, I didn't know if Shawn was serious or not about what he had said in the letter. I kissed him softly goodnight on my front porch and I knew.

You Should be Dancing

If I was worried about anything as my relationship with Shawn transformed into romance, it was that we might lose our friendship. Shawn had been part friend, part brother, and part adviser for years. I didn't want to think about losing all that if things didn't work out for us. That was a minor worry though, and I happily called all my friends and told them that Shawn had asked me to Prom.

I had to worry about getting a dress because I wasn't going to wear the same dress I had worn to Homecoming, but Prom was still a month away, so I had plenty of time to think about that.

We went back to school on Monday and everything seemed normal. We didn't make a big deal out of being a couple, but we did spend more time hanging out in the hallways and at lunch. I don't know if anyone else really noticed anything different about us. Toward the end of the week, Shawn walked down to the freshman end of the hall just before the bell for the next period rang.

"Hey. Kenny Schoenfeld asked me if we wanted to go on a double date with him to some disco in Longview. What do you think? Wanna go?"

I had to stop and think. I didn't really like Kenny. He always seemed full of himself and just a little bit better than everyone else. To me, that probably explained why he only dated girls from out of town; they didn't really know him. Still, it would be fun to go to a disco in Longview, and I would be with Shawn, so I knew everything would be good.

"Yeah, sure. I'll have to check with Mom, but I'm pretty sure I can go."

"Awesome. Let me know if it's a problem. Otherwise, I'll be

over to pick you up about 6:30."

"K... Bye."

I thought for a second that he might give me a quick kiss, but he just smiled at me and ran down the hallway. He had told me he loved me in a letter, but he wasn't ready for a public kiss in the halls of Mossyrock High School.

The trip to Longview started out well. Shawn came over and sat in the living room talking to Mom and Dad for a few minutes before Kenny pulled up in his Nova. We had to drive about twenty minutes to pick up Kenny's date, but he had a super loud sound system in his car that made it impossible to talk.

The disco was called Hollywood Hollywood. I'd never been to a disco before, so I didn't have anything to compare it to, but I was impressed. They had a little room where you could check your jacket and there was a bar where you could order a pop. They also had kid versions of adult mixed drinks, like virgin margaritas. Compared to the sound in the disco, Kenny's car audio system was minor. I could feel the bass vibrating the floor when we danced. The dance floor and walls were lighted, playing patterns in rhythm with the music. We didn't have anything like that in Mossyrock.

We claimed a table and all ordered Cokes, but there was no way to have a conversation, so mostly we danced. After five or six dances, we got so hot that we went outside and stood in the cool night air, then went right back to the dance floor. The whole night at the club went by in a blur of thumping music, flashing lights, and dancing until we were exhausted. I still had a curfew, though, so we left the club before 10 o'clock and headed back to drop off Kenny's date in Onalaska.

Shawn and I rode in the back seat and held hands. I was tired from dancing and happy just to be with him. When we pulled into the driveway where Kenny's date lived, he hopped out and smirked at us in the back seat. He turned the car off but left the key in and turned down the sound. I wondered how long he was planning on being gone.

I glanced over at Shawn to see what he was doing. He was just looking at me. He reached out and touched my face, pulled me to him and kissed me. We held the kiss longer than we ever had before and then he turned in his seat and kissed me harder. It felt like too much. It was kind of overwhelming. I broke away and turned my head, but a minute later we were kissing again. It didn't feel right. I don't think either one of us knew what we were doing. At one point, his tongue licked against the end of my nose, which I was pretty sure wasn't how this was supposed to work.

When he had kissed me after we had gone to see *Star Wars*, it had made my legs go weak, but sitting here in the back seat of Kenny's car, it wasn't the same. Finally, I turned away and looked out the window to take a breather.

When I looked back, Shawn had slid away from me and looked like he wasn't in a very good mood. We could have easily had a conversation, but we didn't. Everything felt wrong. I wondered if I had blown it with Shawn. I had kissed boys before, but it had never been anything like this. If I didn't even know how to make out in the back seat of a car, would he still want me to be his girlfriend?

The car ride back to Mossyrock took forever, and I was miserable the whole way. When we pulled into the driveway between our houses, we both jumped out. I was hoping that maybe we would stand in the yard and talk for a minute, but Shawn just mumbled "good night" and went straight home. When I walked into the house, I thought I had messed up the whole relationship. Maybe Shawn wouldn't want to see me anymore. I wondered if he would decide not to take me to Prom, just like Gordon had decided not to take me to Homecoming. I don't cry a lot, but when I lay down on my bed, I felt like I wanted to.

Over the next few weeks, it felt like a little of the fun and excitement had gone out of whatever my relationship was with Shawn. If I was his girlfriend, he wasn't acting like it. He was still giving me a ride to and from school, but he seemed a lot more distant than he had been before.

I knew that Shawn would be graduating in just a few months and right after that he would be going to Alaska for the summer with Jerry. He had also been accepted at the University of Washington, so he would be off to college at the end of summer. It all gave me an unsettled feeling that I didn't like, but I didn't know how to do anything about it.

On the Friday the week before Prom, he gave me a ride home like always. This time though, when we pulled into the driveway and I started to get out, Shawn said, "Hang on a second."

I looked at him, but I wasn't giving him anything. I was tired of this distance between us. I wondered if he was going to break up with me or tell me we weren't going to Prom after all. If he did that, I would feel completely crushed. Mom would be furious, since we had just gone to Olympia the week before to pick out a dress that matched Shawn's tux.

Instead, he said, "We haven't gone dancing since we went to Longview a while ago. I was thinking maybe we should go again to kind of practice for Prom."

That was silly, of course. We had never practiced before, and we did just fine at Hollywood Hollywood, but that didn't matter. This was the first time in almost a month that he had gone out of his way to spend time with me.

"OK, what are you thinking?"

"I was thinking maybe we could drive down to Longview and go to that same place. It was cool."

He looked a little fearful and uncertain, like maybe I wouldn't want to go with him, so I just nodded and said, "OK."

We decided to leave at 6:00, since I had an 11:00 curfew. When he picked me up, things felt different. I don't know why, but as we drove the forty miles to Longview in the Vega, the weeks of uncertainty and distance faded away. We listened to 62 KGW out of Portland as we drove, and after a few miles on the freeway, Shawn reached over and put his hand on mine.

When we got to Hollywood Hollywood, Shawn took my jacket to the coat check. While he was doing that, I was standing at the edge of the dance floor, listening to the music. A boy about my age walked up and asked me if I wanted to dance. I was about to tell him 'no, thank you' when Shawn appeared out of nowhere. The boy was about my height. Shawn was tall to begin with, and was wearing the same platform shoes he wore for KISS II, which made him about 6'6". He leaned over, got close to the boy's ear and growled something at him. Sometimes I swore he really thought he *was* Gene Simmons. The boy's eyebrows shot up. He didn't say a word but he disappeared in a hurry.

I gave Shawn a glare and said, "Really? Was that necessary?" He looked guilty for about half a second, then smiled and it made me laugh. We found a table right at the edge of the dance floor and watched other people dance for a few minutes. Shawn reached under the table and took my hand in his again. I felt so drawn to him. I had gone out with boys before, but I had never felt what I did right at that moment with Shawn. People were all around us, but it felt like we were all alone.

When the DJ played *Always and Forever*, Shawn just stood up, smiled at me and pulled me out onto the dance floor. We had slow-danced before, at his 16th birthday party and again at Homecoming, but this felt different. As soon as we stepped onto the floor, he pulled me close and looked into my eyes. I felt my breath catch a little and our recent emotional distance vanished. It felt like we were one person, split into two bodies. Everything but Shawn and his blue eyes faded away. When he sent me a letter and told me he loved me, I wasn't sure. When he asked me to Prom, I started to believe. Standing on that dance floor, feeling his presence all around me, I knew.

I knew I loved him. Right at that moment, I wanted to give him everything, every part of my heart. Our eyes never left each other as *Always and Forever* started to fade away. I didn't want this moment, this feeling, to end. The DJ played another slow song, though, so we were able to stay in our little cocoon of love and contentment for a few minutes more. When that song too, faded away, the next song was fast and the floor immediately filled with new dancers that bumped and danced all around us. We didn't care. We weren't ready to let go of that moment yet. We ignored the new beat and clung to each other, still moving in a slow circle, dancing to our own music. Shawn finally seemed to realize what we were doing and bent down. He touched his lips to my ear gently and said "Let's go."

We collected my coat and hurried out of the club. I didn't know where we were going and I didn't care. I was feeling something I had never felt before, and I didn't want the night to end yet. It was just getting dark when we got outside. We got in the Vega and Shawn turned the music on low. He slipped the car into gear and headed for Mossyrock. I wrapped my arms around his and rested my head on his shoulder. The ride home felt like it was over almost before it started.

Eventually, I lifted my head and realized we were almost back to Damron Road. We still had almost an hour until my curfew and I couldn't believe he was taking me home. Just before we got to Damron Road, though, there was a road to the left that went up a steep hill to a little cemetery. He slowed down and turned left up the hill.

I looked at Shawn and started to ask why we were going to a cemetery, then realized I didn't care where we were going as long as we were together. We crested the top of the hill and rolled down the little road that ran alongside the graves and headstones. Shawn had picked the quietest place in Mossyrock for us to park.

We took off our seat belts and slid easily together. I laid my head against his chest and I felt him stroke my hair gently. The radio was playing and the moon shone bright. In the back of Kenny's car a few weeks ago, everything had felt wrong. Here, once again, everything was completely right.

I moved my face just a few inches from his. We were so close I could feel the heat radiating from his body. When I looked in his eyes, I felt our connection all the way through me. I moved the last little bit and kissed him long, slow, and deep. I grabbed the back of his neck and pulled him closer to me, loving the way he felt.

When we broke off, he smiled at me, but didn't say anything. Words weren't needed. Shawn managed to keep one eye on his watch, and a few minutes before my curfew, we drove back down Doss Hill and home. I got out of his car and he held me against him for a long minute before he let me go with one last kiss. It was the perfect ending to our perfect night.

Always and Forever

After our second trip to Hollywood Hollywood, my lingering doubts about where Shawn and I stood were gone. He had been picking me up for school since the beginning of the school year, but now we left the house a little earlier and got to school a little later so that we could drive around the back roads and talk for a few extra minutes every morning.

He usually managed to find an excuse to come down to the freshman end of the hall at least two or three times a day to see me, and we ate lunch together. He was finally a little less shy about us being a couple. He would reach up and touch my hair sometimes, or hold my hand while we walked to class, or even put his arm around me once in a while.

Prom was approaching fast. Shawn had been chosen as part of the Prom Court, so he had to wear the same tuxedo that everyone in the Court wore, cream with a white bow tie and tan ruffles on the shirt. Mom helped me find the perfect dress to match it. My stomach was all butterflies that week. I wasn't nervous anymore about Shawn's feelings toward me—he had erased all those doubts. I was nervous because I wanted to do something on Prom night to show him how I felt about him, but I wasn't sure exactly what to do.

On Prom day, I followed my favorite routine: I slept in. It seemed like I could never get enough sleep. As soon as I woke up, thoughts about Prom jumped into my head. I saw Shawn over in the side yard washing and waxing the Sin Bin, but he just waved at me, so I didn't go talk to him.

We didn't have a shower in the house, so I took a long bath and shaved my legs. My hair wasn't real long, so I didn't try to do anything too fancy with it. I just washed and blow-dried it. By the time Shawn came over to pick me up, I was ready, but Mom told me to stay back in my room. I think she wanted me to make an entrance. That wasn't really my style, but there was no use in arguing with Mom about these things, so I sat in my room doing my nails and listening to music.

I heard voices out in the living room and knew Shawn had to be sitting out there waiting for me. As much as Mom wanted me to make an entrance like in a movie, I just didn't have that in me. Instead, I just walked in and said "Hi."

My entrance was plenty for Shawn. He jumped up, swallowed hard and quietly said, "Wow. You look... great. So beautiful."

I didn't really know what to say to that, so I just said, "You too."

"Really? 'Cause I don't think anyone's ever accused me of being beautiful before."

Wise-ass. I shot him a 'you know what I mean' look.

As we were leaving the house, Shawn said, "Mom wants to see you in your dress and take a picture of us, so we've got to stop there before we leave."

When we walked into the trailer, Shawn's mom was in the kitchen doing dinner prep. Even though he had asked me to go to dinner at the Falls Terrace in Olympia, when it came down to it, Shawn didn't have enough money to do that. Instead, his mom was going to make us dinner and we were going to eat after Prom. I don't think I'd ever eaten dinner after 6:30 in my life, so eating at midnight seemed a little odd to me, but I didn't care when or where we ate. I just wanted to be with Shawn.

Ruth told me I looked beautiful and pulled a chair over in front of the heavy red curtains in front of the sliding glass door. She took a Polaroid of me in the chair with Shawn sitting on the arm. The camera spit the picture out, but we didn't wait around for it to develop before we were in the Vega and heading for school.

We had to get to the dance early, since Shawn was part of the court. Mossyrock did things differently than most schools. They didn't elect a queen and king of the prom. Instead, they had five princesses. Everyone voted; the winner was the queen, and the rest were her court. They didn't vote for the boys, so there was no Prom king.

We got there while the band was still tuning up. All the other members of the court were gathered out in the hallway, trying to figure out exactly what they were supposed to do. The queen and her escort would lead off the dancing and then the rest of the court would join in, but they still hadn't announced who that would be.

I had a few minutes to kill, so I went to the girls' bathroom. I was sitting in a stall when I heard two other members of the court come in. They used the mirrors to touch up their makeup and I heard one say, "I don't know why her dress is that color. That's supposed to be just for the Prom Court." *Meow.* I looked down at my dress and peeked through the crack in the stall. Sure enough, my dress and theirs looked pretty similar. I wondered if I had broken another unwritten Mossyrock rule.

I could have hidden in the stall for a few more minutes and waited for them to leave, but instead I flushed the toilet, opened the door, and walked to the sink to wash my hands. I saw the two girls exchange glances, but I didn't bother saying anything. I just smiled at them sweetly and walked right by without waiting to see their reactions.

I knew it might be a while before Shawn finished his Prom Court duties, so I sat down at one of the big tables in the multipurpose room to wait for him. Soon we would get to spend the rest of the night together. I looked around at the decorations the Prom Committee had set up. There was a throne and smaller chairs at one side of the room, and lots and lots of crepe paper. Small-town formal dances must have kept the crepe paper companies in business for years.

Eventually, the room filled up and all the lights dimmed. Jim Croce's *Time in a Bottle* started to play and Carolyn walked out, having been announced as the Queen of the Prom. She had her arm through Shawn's, who seemed to be squinting into the spotlight, looking for me. Shawn and Carolyn danced alone for just a few seconds, then the rest of the court and their escorts came in and waltzed. As soon as the song ended, the whole Court was whisked over to the throne to take pictures, after which Shawn was free. He rushed over and kissed my cheek and said, "I missed you." I knew that was silly. Still, it made me happy. For Shawn, being silly was the norm, and at times like this it was part of his appeal.

Our Prom was just like every other Prom held in small towns across the country, with cheesy decorations, a cover band playing Top 40 songs louder than necessary, and teenagers who normally wore jeans and tennis shoes dressed up in tuxedos and formal dresses. Still, to Shawn and me, that night felt magical, like anything could happen. Or maybe that something good had already happened and we were there to celebrate it.

This was one of the best nights of my life and it passed like a blur. Shawn and I were surrounded by our friends, but we could only see each other. We danced a lot and made sure we never missed a slow song. It was when the band played their version of Billy Joel's *Just the Way You Are* that I finally knew what I wanted to do to show Shawn I loved him.

When the dance was done, we got in the Vega and drove the mile home. Our ears were still ringing from the music and we might have been perspiring a little bit from dancing so much, but we were happy.

When we pulled into the side yard, everything was dark in my house, but when I looked through the window at Shawn's house, the whole inside was glowing softly. When we walked through the sliding glass door, I saw why. Ruth had put lighted candles all over the living and dining rooms. There were no electric lights on, but I could see the beautiful table she laid out for us.

There was a nice tablecloth with a beautiful arrangement of flowers from her garden as a centerpiece. She had even folded the napkins so they looked just like they did in a nice restaurant. Our plates were already out and they were still hot, so she must have waited until she saw us pull in the driveway before she took everything out of the oven and got out of sight.

On each plate was a Cornish game hen stuffed with wild rice, homemade dinner rolls, and a green salad. There was also a decorative glass that had layers of chocolate pudding and whipped cream.

"Will you tell your mom 'thank you' for doing all this for us?" I asked. "It's so beautiful. This is way better than going out to a restaurant somewhere."

He smiled, reached out, and touched my hair. "I will," he said. He looked so good with the candlelight in his eyes. He took my shawl and pulled my chair out for me. Everything was so elegant and tasted so good, but I wasn't really hungry, so we mostly just pushed the food around on our plates and made small talk. I knew we were approaching the end of the evening, and it was time to put my plan into action.

In the background, I heard *Always and Forever* slowly fade out, then a few seconds of silence and it started again. Shawn's mom must have set the 45 to play on repeat on their stereo.

We stood up from the table and moved into the living room, where I could hear the music more clearly. Shawn was smiling at me in a way that told me he was very happy, but that he thought our night was done. I could understand that since it was almost 1 AM and my usual curfew was 11:00.

In the middle of the living room, I put my hand on his arm to stop him and said, "Wanna dance?"

His eyebrows shot up a little bit, but his smile broadened and he opened his arms wide to welcome me. I took two quick steps and rested my head against his chest, feeling the boundaries between us start to dissolve. He was still wearing his tuxedo, so in reality I rested my head against his jacket, vest, cummerbund and frilly shirt, but no matter. It was still him.

We danced just like we had the week before at Hollywood Hollywood, holding each other close and circling so slowly. I put my arms around him and pulled him so close to me that it started to feel like we were one person, not two. The song ended, but we didn't. In the sudden quiet, we kept moving, dancing along until the music caught up with us again.

I knew what I wanted to do to show Shawn how I felt about him, but I wasn't sure if I had the nerve to carry it out. We danced to *Always and Forever* again and again until finally I knew that if I didn't do it right then, I wouldn't be able to do it at all.

Taking a deep breath, I pushed myself away from Shawn and took two steps back. Feeling the butterflies in my stomach more strongly than ever but trusting Shawn and wanting to do something to show him how I felt, I reached up and pushed my dress off both my shoulders at the same time. I felt it slide away and gather in a small pool at my feet.

Shawn's eyes got huge and he started to sway a little from side to side. I was afraid he might pass out. He took one step toward me, and I thought he might pull me into him again. But instead he held my face in his hands and stared into my eyes for the longest moment of my life. It felt so real, I shivered and felt goose bumps rise, but it was from excitement, not from the cold.

I held my arms out to him, welcoming him as he had welcomed me. He stepped into me and held me tightly against him, me wearing only my bra and panties and him still wearing his entire tuxedo. He took a half step back again like he wanted to both hold me and drink me in. He reached out and touched my face gently and let his hand slide down my neck to my shoulder and pushed my bra strap away. I reached behind me and unhooked it, letting it fall to the ground with my dress.

It felt very odd to be standing in Shawn's living room, almost naked and him still dressed like he was ready to leave for the dance, so I pulled on the lapel of his jacket. We took four or five stumbling steps toward the couch, with Shawn shedding parts of his tuxedo with each step. By the time we made the couch, he was wrestling with his cummerbund.

I lay back against the pillows and marveled at his face in the candlelight. He looked so happy, so in love, it almost made me cry.

I put both arms around his neck and pulled him down to me. I kissed him with every part of me—my heart, my soul, my body.

"Shawn. I love you."

"Dawn Adele, I love you too."

It took a few more twists and turns, but eventually he got completely out of his tux and we lay against each other on the couch with nothing but our skin between us.

I smiled gently at him, then looked as stern as I could manage and said, "But, you know, it's still 'no.'"

I knew I loved him, and looking at him left no doubt that he loved me too, but we were way too young for sex. At the same time, I had just stripped nearly nude in his living room on Prom night, so I knew we needed to talk about it. He smiled too, and then looked serious and nodded.

"It's 'no' for me, too."

And that was that. I wish I could remember what happened for the next few hours, but they seemed to pass in just a few seconds. We lay on the couch, mostly without moving, just enjoying the feeling of holding each other so close. We talked and laughed and stared at each other. I didn't know it was possible to feel so much.

I think we might have stayed on that couch forever if the world hadn't interrupted, but it did. I heard a metallic click and knew immediately what it was: Shawn's mom had opened her bedroom door. We both froze. If she came out into the living room, we were caught.

Instead, the next thing I heard was the happy sound of the bathroom door closing around the corner in the hallway. I jumped up from the couch and grabbed my clothes. We were both scared to death at the thought of being busted, but at the same time, it was kind of funny. I saw a smile pass across Shawn's face as he crawled naked around the floor, trying to gather up the parts of his tux. Before he had managed to get his pants on, I was dressed and holding my shoes in my hand.

I never wanted this night to end, but I knew I had to go. I saw the first rays of sunlight sneaking in around the blinds. Shawn finally gathered up everything he needed in one hand and was trying to hold his pants up with the other, an image I knew would stay in my mind forever. His panic passed and all I saw in his face was love and happiness.

I smiled at him, kissed him softly one last time and walked across the yard to home.

I Just Wanna Stop

When I walked in the front door, Dad was sitting in his easy chair with his morning cup of tea. Although they hadn't wanted to let me stay out past nine o'clock a month before, and it was now a few minutes after 5 AM, I wasn't worried about being in trouble. They knew I was next door, safe, and with Shawn. They trusted him, although I don't know what they thought we were doing all night.

Dad smiled and said, "You look absolutely lovely. How is it you manage to look so beautiful after such a long night?"

I answered truthfully and with one word.

"Shawn."

I didn't want any more conversation to interrupt everything I was feeling, so I just said "'Night," and made a beeline to the bathroom. I was out of my Prom dress again, in my comfy jammers and in bed in less than two minutes. I wanted to continue to ride the high I was feeling from spending those hours on the couch with Shawn, but happy dreams were irresistible and sleep pulled me in.

Many years later, Dad gave me a poem called *Dawn* that he wrote that morning after I went to bed. I guess a lot of parents would have yelled at their fourteen-year-old daughter for coming home at sunrise after a dance, but mine wrote a poem about how happy I looked.

The week before, I had been worried about what future I might have with Shawn—what would happen after graduation, how long he would be gone to Alaska, whether we would still be together when he went to college—but that had all faded away. Stripping ourselves naked in front of each other—in more ways than one—removed any doubts or fears I had. It was still hard for me to believe that I'd worked up the courage to drop my dress like that, but I trusted Shawn. I trusted him not to go any farther than I wanted, but even more, I trusted him not to blab. Mossyrock was a very small town where everyone definitely knew everyone else's business. If Shawn told any of his friends what we did when we were alone, my reputation would be gone forever. He never did, at least until it was too late for secrets.

With just a month between Prom and graduation, it felt like a clock was constantly ticking our hours away. We spent every possible minute together. We started leaving for school earlier and earlier and getting to school later and later. We drove the back roads and listened to music until just before the first period bell rang. After school, I met Shawn by the Vega and we rode home together. I would hurry through whatever chores I had, then meet him in the yard. Most of the time we couldn't go anywhere on a school day, but it didn't matter. Just like when we first became friends, we would sit cross-legged on the grass and talk until Mom called me in for dinner.

As soon as I had eaten dinner, I would go to my room and call Shawn on the princess phone that hung on the wall above my bed. We probably would have talked until it was time to go to bed if it was up to us, but that was usually impossible. Shawn's family was on a party line, sharing a phone line with three other people on Damron Road. Sometimes when they picked up the phone, instead of getting a dial tone, they heard other people talking. Of course, that meant that when Shawn and I were talking, we would sometimes hear the little click that told us that someone else was on the line. If that happened, the polite thing to do was to put the phone back down and try again later. We knew that the little old lady two houses down did not do the polite thing. What she thought she might hear in the endless conversations of two teenagers, I have no idea. Eventually, out of nowhere, we would hear, "You kids get off the phone, now. I've got a call to make," and that would be the end of our night's call.

We also wrote each other notes. With texting, instant messages and cell phones, I fear that today's kids will never know the thrill of getting a folded piece of paper slipped to them between classes. After Prom, we wrote each other those notes every day and we would both sign them "Forever." Eventually, we dropped the quotation marks and just started signing them—

Forever. Looking back on it, that seems hopelessly juvenile, but at the time it felt very meaningful to us, like we were crossing another bridge.

As much time as we spent together, I shouldn't have been too surprised that Mom was beginning to think it was all too much.

"You haven't seen much of your friends lately, have you?" or "Don't you think you two are seeing a little too much of each other?" became familiar refrains from her. I ignored them though, and she mostly ignored the fact that I was ignoring her. Shawn's trip to Alaska loomed like a definite deadline ahead of us. From her point of view, the problem would soon go away.

We had both decided on Prom night that, as intimate as we were, neither of us was ready for sex. I wanted to be a virgin on my wedding night, and I knew that was years and years away. That was easy for me to remember most of the time, except when we climbed that hill back up to Doss Cemetery and parked in our spot. We would open the back hatch of the Vega, take turns undressing each other, and lay under the moon and stars naked for the world to see. Most nights that was enough, and I felt so close to Shawn that it was almost like we shared one mind. Other nights though, just lying naked in the moonlight didn't feel like enough. We would take turns encouraging each other that it would be all right if we just did it once. Luckily for my virginity pledge, we never both got the fever at the same time and the cooler head always prevailed.

This intimacy might have caused us to lose perspective on public displays of affection—and how my mom might react. One night in late May, after sitting out in the yard and talking, Mom called me in for dinner. As usual, Shawn walked me to my door. As we walked past the Vega, he twirled me around and into him. We lay back against the side of the car and I rested my head on his chest. I felt content and happy, just like I always did when we were this close. I don't know how long we stayed like that, maybe two or three minutes. I knew Mom would be getting impatient for me to come in for dinner though, so I gave Shawn a lingering kiss and ran for home.

Mom didn't say anything to me when I got inside, but I could tell she was upset about something. After school the next day, she called Shawn and me on the carpet.

"What I witnessed last night has greatly upset me. After I called you in to dinner, I saw you two acting like a couple of animals. I'm sure the whole neighborhood saw. It was inappropriate and it will not happen again. Is that understood?"

I glanced at Shawn, who looked surprised. Neither of us had thought that a kiss and hug in the yard was wrong, but we both nodded and mumbled "OK." As I look back now, this seems to have been a turning point. There was a change in Mom's attitude toward Shawn and me. Before this, she often encouraged me to spend time with Shawn: at Homecoming, with tutoring, whatever. Now it felt like I crossed an invisible line, and she was letting me know it.

We ignored these warning signs, though, and continued to spend every minute together that we could. We were young, we made each other happy, and that's all we thought about. I was a steady young girl, never too excited and never too sad. I had always felt like I had been waiting for something to come along, something that might bring out everything I had inside. Finding and falling in love with Shawn did that, and I didn't question it.

At Mossyrock High School, they let the senior class out a week before graduation. Shawn took a job working on a farm outside of town, and that meant I was back to either walking to school or riding the bus. After a year of riding to school with Shawn, it was hard to get back on the bus, but that's how it would be going forward. When school started again, Shawn would be off to college, and I would be alone again on Damron Road.

The closer it got to graduation, the heavier things felt between us. Then Shawn caught strep throat a couple of days before graduation. We decided we weren't going to go to his senior party since I wouldn't have been able to stay like all the seniors. I figured instead that we would take one last trip up to Doss Cemetery and find that feeling we always did there. Instead, he was too sick to even do that. We were both home in our beds while the other grad parties were just getting started.

Shawn and Jerry were scheduled to leave for Alaska two days after graduation. Shawn had gone to Alaska three times before to spend the summers with his brother. He'd had so many adventures and made so much money there, it must have been irresistible to plan one last trip with his best friend before college separated them. By graduation, Shawn was having second thoughts, but after having planned the trip for almost a year, he felt like he had to go. I knew he would rather spend the summer seeing me, but he didn't want to back out on Jerry.

The day before he left, we naturally spent the whole day together. We didn't do much of anything, because he was still just getting over his strep throat and he needed to save whatever money he had to support himself in Alaska until he got a job. We spent a lot of the day sitting in Shawn's bedroom listening to music. He had gotten a Beatles album as a graduation present, and we listened to it over and over that day. Normally, I wouldn't have been allowed in Shawn's room, but his mom cut us some slack because he was leaving the next day. Plus, we made sure we left the door open and she kept popping her head in every few minutes to check on us. That was fine, because we felt too sad to fool around that day.

We were sitting at opposite ends of his twin bed with our legs tangled in the middle, listening to music and not talking much, when Shawn sat up.

"Dawn." He looked so serious.

"What? I'm still right here."

"I can't stand the thought of being without you. I've never felt anything like what I've felt with you this last month. I have to go to Alaska, 'cuz there's no way to get out of it now, but when I get back, I don't want us to be separated anymore. I just want to be with you."

"Yeah, me too. But as soon as you get back, won't you be leaving for UW?"

"Yeah." He slumped back against his pillow, defeated. "But still… as soon as we can, I want us to be together all the time."

I wasn't completely sure what he was talking about, but I think he was saying he wanted us to get married eventually. How very Shawn it was: implying it without knowing how to blurt it out. "That's what I want too." I reached out and grabbed his hand and held it. I knew that moment couldn't last forever, but I sure wanted it to.

Late that afternoon, we drove the few miles to Lake Mayfield to see my friend Cindi Cowan. I don't know why we decided to do that, because we'd never gone together to see her before. Shawn, Cindi and I walked along the lake and talked for a long time before we went into her house.

Cindi sat down at the piano in her living room and started playing. Eventually, she played *The Love Theme from Romeo and Juliet.* I hadn't lost all perspective, so I knew that Shawn leaving for three months wasn't anything like the famous story. Even so, listening to Cindi play the song felt so sad and haunting that I couldn't stop a few tears from spilling over. I held on to Shawn's hand as tight as I could, and when I looked up at him, I saw tears in his eyes too.

When the last note of the song faded away, we looked outside and saw that it was starting to get dark. We had done our best to stretch out every moment, but our last day together was done.

Magnet and Steel

When I woke up the next morning, Shawn was gone to Alaska. He and Jerry had left for the airport in the middle of the night. I looked out my window and saw the Vega still sitting in its normal place between our two yards, but I knew it would just be sitting there for a long time.

I walked out and plopped down on the couch. Mom said, "I think Shawn left you some things." She pointed to a little pile of stuff on the coffee table.

"Where was it?"

"Dad said he found it out on the front porch this morning when he went to work."

On the top of the pile was a little homemade envelope. Shawn had taken two pieces of lined notebook paper and stapled them all around on three sides. On the front, he had handwritten the lyrics to *Always and Forever*. Inside, he had put his 45 of the song. Underneath that was an identical envelope he had made, but this time the lyrics and 45 were of Peter, Paul & Mary's version of *Leavin' on a Jet Plane*. Maybe it was my imagination, but it seemed like he had taken extra care in writing the words, "When I come back, I'll wear your wedding ring."

At the bottom of the little pile was a blue school notebook. On the cover, Shawn had written *DAWN ADELE* in bold letters. When I opened the notebook, I found page after page of his handwriting, like he had written me one last mega-note.

I scooped it all up and headed for my bedroom so I could listen to the songs and read the notebook in private, although I was pretty sure Mom had already read it all before I woke up. She said, "I know he's gone, but somehow it feels like he never left." I ignored her, but she kept on. "I'm sure you're going to miss him, but it will be good for you to have a little separation. You'll have to get used to it soon anyway, when he goes off to college."

Hearing Mom say exactly what I had been thinking didn't help at all, so I didn't answer except to turn on my heel and go to my room. I put *Always and Forever* on repeat on my little stereo, laid down on my bed, and opened the notebook.

Dawn Adele –
When I think about you, I always hear music, so I wanted to list some of the songs we've listened to and why they will always make me think of you.

The first song he had listed was *Magnet and Steel* by Walter Egan. He wrote that he first heard that song when he was giving me a ride to school, before we started dating. Even so, he said it would always remind him of me, no matter where he was when he heard it. Then he listed dozens of the other songs we had listened to, and why they would always be part of our story to him. He must have stayed up all night working on it.

I spent a few hours sitting on my bed, reading the little book Shawn had written for me and feeling blue while listening to our songs. Eventually, I realized it was summer outside. The weather was nice and the world was going to keep spinning whether I participated or not. So I hauled myself outside, saddled up my horse Rocky, and went for a ride up to Mossyrock.

We had a pigeon named Fred. He lived in a coop, but we let him come and go as he pleased. Sometimes he flew along behind Dad when he went to work. When he did that, Dad was afraid he wouldn't be able to find his way home, so he would put Fred in the car until it was time to go home.

I was about halfway up Damron Road when I saw Fred flying along behind me. Eventually, he caught up and landed on Rocky's hindquarters. For the rest of the trip, we made a nice little parade—me, Rocky and Fred.

By the time I got home, I was still a little sad and missing Shawn, but things seemed better than when I woke up that morning. It was still a little weird, riding past the Sin Bin and seeing it sitting there, quiet and forgotten.

Within a few days, I started my new job at DeGoede's bulb farm. Dad had gotten me the job, which didn't excite me too much; it was really hard work for $2.35 an hour. But Mom told me that if I wanted new clothes for school, I had to earn the money myself. I couldn't picture myself showing up in the same clothes I wore my freshman year, so I took the job.

People who have never farmed have no idea how backbreaking it can be. Every day I walked down rows of bulbs, bent down, pulled them up, and put them in a gunny sack I drug along behind me. When my bag was full, I carried it to a drop-off, emptied it, and started all over again. When it was sunny, you'd think I'd have gotten a tan, but it's hard to get a tan through all the layers of dirt. I never did learn to love the job, especially the part where I got up earlier in the summer than I did when I went to school, but I stuck with it.

About a week after Shawn left, he called me from a payphone in Kodiak.

"Hey, baby… I miss you so much."

"I miss you too, a lot," I said.

I was surprised he'd been able to call because long distance calls from Alaska were so expensive. Hearing his voice just made me miss him more.

"Things aren't going very well up here. The jobs on the fishing boat that we thought we had fell through. We're sleeping on the boat, but it's in dry-dock and it doesn't have any power or water on it. I haven't had a shower in a week. We got a job working on a fish refinery, though, so it's OK, it's just not what we were expecting. How are you doing, baby?"

"I'm fine. Just working at DeGoede's every day and missing you. I wish you were here."

"I wish I was there even more. I was hoping that when I was up here and working that the days would fly by, but every day it's a little bit harder to stay up here without you."

A recorded voice interrupted. "Please deposit two dollars and twenty five cents for another three minutes."

"Aw, crap. I'm out of quarters. Almost out of money altogether. Hope we get paid soon."

"Shawn, I love you."

"Dawn Adele…"

I knew he was about to tell me he loved me, too, but he got cut off, so I never got to hear it. When I sat the phone down in the cradle, I saw Mom staring at me.

"It's going to be hard to miss him if he can't stay away."

"No, it's not, Mom, I do miss him every day."

She muttered something, but I didn't hear it because I was busy slamming the screen door as I went outside. I walked over to the Vega and sat down, leaning my back against it.

I had hoped Shawn would call and talk to me at least a few times over the summer, but now I knew that hearing his voice only made things worse. It felt like tearing the scab off a cut and now it needed to start healing all over again.

A few days later, I asked Cindi Cowan to come spend the night with me. I felt better when I had someone to talk to, and Cindi was a good listener. We were all eating dinner when the phone rang. My stomach flipped a little. Was Shawn calling me again already? Was everything all right? I jumped up from the table and ran to the phone, ignoring the dirty look from Mom.

I picked up the heavy black handset and said "Hello?"

"Well, hello!"

It wasn't Shawn. "Who's this?"

"Isn't that just the way it is? I call a pretty girl up to ask her on a date and all she can say is 'Who is this.' Story of my life."

It was Tommy, Shawn's nephew from Auburn.

"Oh, hey Tommy. What are you doing?"

"Nothing right now, but I'm going to be rolling into the 'Rock sometime tomorrow and I wonder if you would like to accompany me to that disco you guys go to down in Longview?"

"Did Shawn put you up to this?"

"He may have…"

"K. Hang on just a sec."

I put my hand over the mouthpiece and turned around to Mom, still at the table. "Tommy is coming down from Auburn tomorrow and he's going to take me to Longview to go dancing."

I didn't wait for a response, but just said "OK, see you tomorrow night," and hung up. When I sat back down, Mom's mouth was a thin line and her eyes were narrow.

"I didn't tell you that you could go, did I?"

I stared back, but didn't say anything. I thought she was ticked off at me because I had just assumed I could go and now wanted to threaten me with not going.

She was quiet for a minute and said, "Did Shawn put him up to this?"

I nodded.

"Well, if Shawn trusts him to take care of you, I do too. You can go."

I glanced at Cindi out of the corner of my eye, but tried to keep the smile off my face and out of my voice. Cindi saw it and shot me a quick smile.

"Thanks."

"Same rules apply. Home by eleven."

"I know."

I didn't think that would be a problem, since Tommy and I wouldn't be going up to Doss Cemetery on the way home.

The next day at DeGoede's dragged on worse than usual. Seeing Tommy wasn't the same as seeing Shawn, but we had become friends and I knew we would have a good time. Summer was off to a boring, hard-working start, and this would be something different.

Because we started work at DeGoede's so early, I also got off early. I was home, cleaned up and ready to go by 4:30, since I didn't know exactly what time Tommy was going to pick me up.

A little after dinner, Tommy knocked on the door. He sat down on the couch in the same place Shawn sat so often when he came to visit. It was a little like he was a replacement Shawn for the day.

Mom had been working on this weird project, and now she hauled it out and showed it to Tommy. She had taken a roll of toilet paper and painstakingly written a whole series of little jokes on it. It was like the 1978 version of posting something on your Facebook wall, I guess. She called it Colleen's Bathroom Humor and had been working on it ever since Shawn had left for Alaska. Her plan was to fill the whole roll with her jokes and observations and give it to Shawn as a 'going away to college' gift when he got back from Alaska.

She hauled it out and unrolled everything she had written on it, showing it to Tommy.

"I'm going to have it all filled before he gets home," she said.

"I don't know about that," Tommy said. That was an odd thing for him to say, but I was just happy to see him, so I ignored it.

Just then, I heard a horn honking outside. It reminded me of the Vega, a sound I knew quite well. When I listened to the pattern of the honking, I knew what it was. Whenever I was supposed to meet Shawn out at the Vega to go somewhere, he would honk out the rhythm to *Love Gun* on his horn to let me know he was there. He thought it was funny. I'm pretty sure the rest of Damron Road could have wrung his neck.

Now, I was hearing the rat-a-tat-tat of *Love Gun* again, but I couldn't figure out why someone would do that. The weirdest image crossed my mind of Shawn's step-dad Robert sitting behind the wheel of the Vega honking the horn, but I knew that couldn't be right.

I jumped up and threw open the front door and screen door to see who was messing with me. There was a big bush that grew beside our front porch and one of its limbs had grown out so that I couldn't immediately see the Vega. When I pushed the branch out of the way, I saw Shawn leaning up against the Vega, smiling at me.

In two seconds I was in his arms again. He looked and smelled so good, just like he was supposed to. I didn't want to let go of him, but eventually I did and said, "What are you doing here?"

His eyes sparkled. "I told you I missed you. I just couldn't let this time that we could be together get away from us."

"Yay!"

Yes, I actually said ' yay ' like a little girl who has just been handed a double scoop ice cream cone. Shawn brought that out in me. Tommy had wandered out from the outside and slapped Shawn on the back.

"Thanks, bro," said Shawn.

"You two set this all up, didn't you?"

"Yep."

"I hate you sometimes."

"Really? I left Alaska two months early just to see you and now you hate me? I'm crushed." He didn't look crushed. He looked tremendously pleased with himself.

"Are we still going to Hollywood Hollywood?" I asked.

Shawn looked at Tommy. "Of course. Let's go!"

"Wait, we've got to talk to Mom first. I know she'll want to see you."

Walking across the yard holding hands with Shawn was one

of the best feelings I ever had. All the loneliness and boredom of the summer had vanished with the honk of the Vega's horn.

A lot of that happiness went away as soon as we walked in the living room. Mom had tucked away the roll of jokes she had been showing Tommy. Now she looked stern, with her arms crossed and her eyes narrowed.

"So, you're home," she said.

"Yep," Shawn said, smiling. As he noticed Mom's sour expression, the smile faded and he raised his eyebrows at me. I shook my head slightly, because I had no idea why she was suddenly in a bad mood.

"And why did you come home so early? I thought you weren't going to be back until August."

"Well, that was the plan, but the plan changed."

"What changed, exactly?"

"I guess I got homesick and just decided to come home."

"What are you going to do now that you're home?"

Shawn cocked his head to the side, like he was trying to figure out where this onslaught of questions was coming from. For my part, I just stood there, hoping the three of us could get away and go have fun together.

"I just touched down yesterday, so I don't have a plan yet. I figure people will always need help on their farms, spraying for weeds and shoveling horse crap, plus haying season will be here soon and I know a lot of people will need help then. I'll find something, I always do."

"That's fine, but there are a couple of things I need to let you both know. We were very lenient with Dawn the last few months; letting her stay out late and letting you two spend all day, every day together. We chose to do that because we knew you were about to graduate, and head off to Alaska and then college. We wanted you two to be able to enjoy yourselves while you could. But, now that you've come back so early, things are going to be different."

Shawn glanced over at me, looking serious. His expression said: *I have stepped in a mess that I didn't even see coming.*

"For one, we will have rules and curfews and you will follow them to the letter. For another, you will not be spending all your time together this summer. It's not healthy. If you aren't able to keep to these rules, or if you miss curfew, or we think you are spending too much time together, then we won't let you see each other at all."

Those last words just kind of hung there in the air. That seemed so unbelievable I didn't even want to think about it.

"I hope you both are hearing what I am saying, because if you aren't, there will be consequences, and neither one of you will like what they are."

I could feel my face getting hot and I just wanted to get out of there.

"Can we go?" I asked.

"I already told you that you could go tonight, so yes, you can, but don't plan on doing anything else together for a few days."

Shawn, Tommy and I walked out into the front yard, a little stunned. Shawn was the first to recover. "Hey, that was fun. I don't think we can match that by going to Hollywood Hollywood, but let's give it a try, OK?"

He took my hand, led me over to the Vega and opened my door while Tommy climbed in the back. We did have fun that night, because we always did when we were together, but there was a feeling of dread hanging over everything.

Mom never did finish the roll of jokes and she never mentioned it again.

Every Time You Go Away

When Shawn showed up so unexpectedly, I thought my blah summer was going to be great after all. And there were times when it was, but mostly, one thing after another went wrong.

I still had my job at DeGoede's Bulb Farm, so I was getting up early every day and was tired every night. Shawn was looking for work every day, but Mossyrock was a small town and he was a few weeks behind in the summer job hunt. He'd been working at a farm before graduation, but he'd quit when he went to Alaska and they had hired someone else. There were a lot of farms that would need help harvesting their hay come July and August, but that was weeks away. So most days, I was picking bulbs at DeGoede's and he was just over at his house, reading.

The weekends were good though, at least at first. Because I was working a lot, I didn't really have to worry about Mom being on Shawn and me for spending too much time together, and she was fine with us going places on the weekends.

I was saving my money to buy new school clothes, so I didn't even cash my checks as I got them. I just gave them to Mom and she put them in a drawer for me to cash at the end of the summer. That meant, like Shawn, I didn't have any money. Still, every once in a while he was able to find someone who needed an extra hand for the day building a fence, or clearing blackberry bushes off a hillside or something, and then he would have a few dollars. When that happened, we would escape Mossyrock and go to a movie in Centralia, or to Hollywood Hollywood, or just go for a drive.

Shawn's stepbrother Russell and stepsister Tylene had come to spend part of the summer in Mossyrock. Russell was a year older than me, and Ty was a year younger. Whenever I wasn't working and we were all broke, we all hung out together. We probably played a thousand games of Yard Darts, badminton and Crazy Eights together that summer.

Things started to go bad about three weeks after Shawn got back. I was in my bedroom listening to music and Shawn, Russ and Ty were in their yard throwing a Frisbee around. I opened my window and turned my music up a little louder so they could hear it. Eventually they quit tossing the Frisbee and came over to my window to talk to me.

It was about as innocent as it could be. We were just talking about whether Shawn had enough gas in the Vega to get us all down to Ike Kinswa State Park so we could go swimming, when my bedroom door flew open and Mom walked in, looking royally ticked off. Even though it was almost lunch time, she had apparently been trying to sleep in her bedroom, which was right next to mine. The combination of my music and us talking woke her up.

"This is too much. Dawn, come with me. I want to talk to you."

I didn't feel like we had done much wrong, so I shrugged, waved goodbye and followed her into the living room. She sat down in her chair and fixed me with the look that told me I was in some kind of trouble.

"We tried to talk to you about this, but you don't seem to be getting the message. You are still spending entirely too much time with Shawn."

"But…"

"No, no 'buts.' The fact that you didn't bother to think about whether or not I might be laying down because I'm not feeling well is just a symptom of all the rest of this. So, for three days, you are not allowed to see Shawn at all. Not in person, not on the phone, nothing. No contact at all for three days."

"What? Why?" I knew my voice was louder than it should be and a little shrill, but this punishment seemed so out of proportion to the crime of playing my music too loud.

"I already told you and I won't explain myself again. If you want to argue more about it, we can make it a week."

"Ugh! Fine. Whatever. Can I go tell Shawn that?"

"That's fine. Be back in the house in two minutes."

I ran outside and found the three of them still standing

around the yard, talking and laughing. Shawn reached out his hand for mine and grinned at me when he saw me coming. "Well, did you get in trouble?"

"Yes, actually, I did."

"What, seriously? For what?"

"For waking Mom up, I guess. I can't see you or talk to you for three days now. I've got to go back in so she doesn't make it a week. I'm sorry. I'll miss you."

I turned back toward the house and took a few steps when Shawn caught up to me. "It'll be OK," he said. "It sucks, and I don't get it, but it will be OK. I love you."

He hugged me and I felt good again for a minute, but I knew I had to get inside, so I broke away and ran home. I felt awful that he had flown home from Alaska just to see me, and now we couldn't. I was mad at Mom for being so unreasonable, and I felt a little guilty. When Shawn and I were together, he always treated me as his equal, but being punished like this reminded me that we weren't equal in the eyes of other people. He was eighteen. He had graduated and was getting ready to go off to college. I was fourteen and hadn't even started my sophomore year of high school. We might act like we were in the same place, but I knew we weren't.

The three days passed, and life went on just like it had before. Mom still let me see Shawn and go places when we could manage it, but it felt like she was always watching us. One Saturday afternoon, we went down to the lake to swim and lost track of the time. I was supposed to be home at 5:00, but it was closer to 5:30 when we got there. Mom was standing in the front window looking out when we pulled in the yard.

"I think it'll be better if I just go in alone," I said.

"No, I'll go too. Whatever's up, I'd rather be there with you," Shawn said.

When we walked in, Mom said "Shawn, I'm glad you came in, because this involves you too. Dawn's father and I have tried to be very clear with both of you, but you don't seem to be getting the message."

"Honestly, I'm not sure what message we're supposed to be getting," Shawn said. "I'm sorry I brought Dawn home late today, and that's my fault. But, we were just down at the lake with our friends. None of us had a watch, which is no excuse, I know, but we weren't doing anything wrong."

"The message that you should be getting and are not is that we think you two are seeing too much of each other. You're too serious. Dawn is only fourteen and still has three years of school left. You'll be gone to Seattle soon…"

"…and that's why we're hoping to spend as much time together as we can this summer," interrupted Shawn. "We both know I'm going to be gone for months at a time soon."

"Here's the thing I think you're missing, Shawn. This isn't a debate. We are not going to argue with you. You two are forbidden from seeing each other for a week. After that, if you can be together a reasonable amount of time and be home when you are supposed to, you can see each other again. If you can't do that, you will not be allowed to see each other at all."

I couldn't keep silent any longer. "At all? That makes no sense. We haven't done anything wrong, and you're going to stop us from seeing each other?"

"That's exactly what we're going to do. You might keep that in mind from now on. Shawn, it's time for you to go to your own home."

I saw his shoulders sag. He knew he wasn't going to win this argument. He looked at me and I saw the pain in his eyes. "Bye, baby. I'll see you in a week. We'll just be more careful from now on."

And we were careful. Once the week passed, we were on our best behavior. Sometimes a day would go by when I was working and Shawn was haying and we wouldn't see each other at all. One Saturday night, things came together so that we could go to Hollywood Hollywood in Longview again. We hadn't seen each other much over that week, so we were just glad to be together, lost in the sea of dancing couples. When we left the disco, we checked the time. We had stayed a little longer than we had meant to, but that just meant that we wouldn't be able to go up to Doss Cemetery and park. We still had plenty of time to get home.

Whenever we were in the car, my favorite thing to do was to lean over and put my head against Shawn and wrap my arms around his. With the music on and feeling him so near me, I would close my eyes and drift away. It felt like nothing could ever go wrong.

After we'd been in the car for twenty minutes or so, I heard

Shawn say "Oh, crap."

I was instantly wide awake and sat up straight in my seat. Everything looked perfectly normal. "What's wrong?" "When we got on the freeway, I must have got on going south instead of north. All this time, we've been going toward Portland instead of home. We're gonna be late."

We took the next off-ramp and immediately got back on going the right direction. Shawn pushed the Vega over eighty all the way home, but it didn't matter. We both knew we were going to be late. My stomach was in knots, but my curfew passed when we were just getting off I-5 and still twenty minutes away from home.

"When we get home, I'll go in and explain what happened. I think it's better if they hear it from both of us," Shawn said.

I said "OK," but when we pulled into the parking spot, my house was completely dark. There was no use in Shawn coming in. He walked me to my door and I gave him a kiss goodbye. I didn't know when or if I would be seeing him after that. I let myself in, half expecting Mom to be sitting there in the dark waiting for me, but she wasn't. The whole house was quiet, so I got undressed and went to bed. It took me a long time to fall asleep, but I finally did.

I had been asleep a few hours when Dad threw my door open, turned my light on and started yelling. He was shouting so loudly that I really couldn't tell what he was saying. I could hear Mom yelling in the living room too, though, so I knew something was really wrong. I thought that the house was on fire. I jumped out of bed and into some jeans so I could go outside.

When I ran into the living room, Mom yelled, "What time did you get home?"

I couldn't believe it. I looked at the clock on the wall and saw that it was a little after three in the morning. They had waited until I had gone completely to sleep so they could wake me up and yell at me. I wanted to yell right back, but I was tired and disoriented and guilty because I knew we had been late. Instead of yelling, I said quietly, "We got home at 11:20." I was hoping that if I spoke quietly, she would too. It didn't work.

"And, what time were you supposed to be home?"

"11:00."

Her voice became completely calm. "What did I tell you

79

would happen if you were late coming home again?"

I didn't answer. I was through playing this game. The sick feeling in my stomach told me I already knew how this was going to turn out. Mom raised her eyebrows at me like she was waiting for me to say something.

"If it's all right, I'm going back to bed."

"That's fine." She looked meaningfully at Dad, and he nodded at her. "You go back to sleep. But, I want you to know you won't be seeing Shawn any more, at all."

I really couldn't believe it, but I also knew nothing was going to change her mind. I turned around and went to bed. Lying there in the dark, I thought I might cry, but I didn't. I could understand grounding me if I did something wrong, but telling me that I could never see Shawn again? That seemed too impossible to be true. It took me a long time to fall asleep again.

When I woke up the next morning, it was like the blowup in the middle of the night had never happened. Everything was calm and quiet. Mom and Dad said, "Good morning," as if they hadn't just been yelling at me a few hours before. I figured that the best strategy would be to lay low, so I got dressed, made my breakfast, and tried to stay out of the way.

A little before lunch, there was a knock on the door. I could see Shawn through the window. I shot a questioning look at Mom.

"You might as well let him in," she said. "Let's get this over with."

I opened the door. It didn't look like Shawn had slept very well either. His hair was even messier than usual and his eyes looked tired.

As soon as he was inside, Mom said, "Sit down," pointing to the couch. I sat down beside him, because I knew what was coming and that it might be a long time until I saw him again.

"Shawn, we've already told Dawn this, but now we want to tell you. We have given you opportunity after opportunity to follow our rules, but you have not been able to do so. We feel that we do not have any choice now. You will not be allowed to see Dawn anymore."

"Ever?" Shawn's voice rose.

"Ever. We warned you about this and now it is here. We wish we hadn't been forced to do this, but we feel that we have."

He looked so hurt and stunned that I wanted to take him in my arms and hold him, but I knew that wouldn't make the situation any better. Instead, I just reached out and took his hand. The pain in his voice was wrenching: "I don't know what to say. I just can't believe you are doing this."

He stood up and I saw tears in his eyes, threatening to spill over. He shook his head at Mom and Dad, reached out and touched my cheek and walked out.

I didn't say a word. I went to my room, shut the door, and didn't come out for the rest of the day.

Living Inside Myself

My first plan was to stay in my room forever. I couldn't believe Mom and Dad really wouldn't let me see Shawn again. If I didn't have a chance to see him over the next month or two, he would be gone to Seattle and UW. That was a good two hours from Mossyrock. I knew there were a lot of pretty girls there, and it hurt so badly to think about Shawn being with them instead of me. Mostly, though, it just hurt to be without Shawn. He was my best friend, and without him, I didn't even know who to talk to about missing him.

Like all teenagers do, I eventually figured out that I couldn't live on my anger and hurt feelings. I had to come out of my room and face my parents. When I did, things felt different. Ever since Shawn had come back from Alaska, our home had been tense. Today, Mom and Dad were laughing and talking and acting relaxed, like some horrible event was finally behind them. If they noticed my gloomy attitude, they didn't let on.

With Shawn off limits, it felt like there was nothing ahead except work, sleep and boredom. I went to the cabinet where Mom had been keeping my summer paychecks and added them all up. I realized there was already more than enough there to get all the school clothes I would need, with money left over. As soon as I figured out that I didn't need any more money, I was ready to quit, but Mom and Dad wouldn't hear of it.

Later that week, I came up with a way to stop working at DeGoede's without actually quitting. We were getting to the end of the season, when temporary summer workers started to get laid off and the competition for jobs got fiercer. Instead of working harder, my friend Devi and I took it easy one morning, goofing around and spending more time talking than actually working.

Before lunch time, Mr. DeGoede found us in the field and told us that he was sorry, but they were making more cuts and he was going to have to let us go. Since it was the middle of the day, I didn't have a ride home, but I didn't mind walking the few miles home.

A few days later, Dad drove us to Olympia to the M&N Outlet store to do my school shopping. I was excited because I was able to get the Hash jeans I had been wanting. I even had enough money to buy a rabbit fur coat. I really don't know why I bought that coat, other than I thought it was so beautiful at the time. I don't know how many rabbits gave their fur for that coat, and I would never think of buying something like that again, but I loved it at the time.

Something kind of important happened to me during those weeks between being laid off at DeGoede's and starting school, invisible to everyone but me. It felt like I had to split myself in two and begin to choose what to show the world and what to keep inside. The problem was, I loved Shawn and I missed him so much, every day. I couldn't let that show at home, or I would get in trouble for showing too much attitude. My friends would listen sympathetically for a while, but it got pretty old for them too. So, I decided I would keep what I really felt to myself and show a happier face to the rest of the world. It was easy to start doing that, but so, so hard to stop.

School started again in September, and I went out for the volleyball team. One advantage of a very small school—which I would not have had in California—was that nearly everyone could participate in sports, band, and whatever other extracurricular activities existed. I liked playing and feeling like I was part of a team. Games were my best times to forget how down I felt most of the time. During one of our games, Dad showed up and talked to my coach. He told her I had to come out of the game and go with him, right then.

As we were walking to the car, I asked, "Is Mom OK? What's going on?"

"Your Mom's fine, but we've got to go somewhere and we didn't want to leave without you. Your Mom will tell you more when we get in the car."

As soon as I got inside, Mom said, "Your cousin Lori has run away from home. She says she's getting hit at home and things are too bad for her to stay there, so we're going to go pick her up and bring her home to live with us."

That's the way things are sometimes; change happens so fast. One minute I'm in the gym, ready to dig out a spike in a volleyball game, and the next minute I'm on my way to Sumner to pick up my niece to come live with us. You've got to roll with the changes.

It wasn't bad having Lori at our house. It was nice to have someone my own age always around to talk to, and I trusted her. I tested her first by telling her something small, but when I found out she could keep a secret, I told her more. Eventually, I figured out that she had my back and I could tell her pretty much anything.

Even so, there was competition between us. Lori was really skinny, and I felt like I was fatter than I wanted to be, even though I only weighed about 115 lbs. Also, where I was shy and had a hard time talking to people, Lori was outgoing and made new friends easily.

When she first got to school, she had a boyfriend named Roy who was from Sumner, where she used to live. Even though that was an hour and a half away, he still came down to see her quite a bit and usually brought a friend or his brother along. When he did, we would usually all go out on a double date. It made Mom happy, because she thought that meant that I was getting over Shawn. My ability to hide my true feelings was improving.

When we double-dated, we would go to the bowling alley in Mossyrock or to a movie out town. I tried not to, but I couldn't help but compare those dates to what it was like when Shawn and I went out. There was nothing wrong with those boys or what we did, but I never felt anything like that sense of connection I always felt with Shawn.

About that same time, my English teacher, Mr. Bartee, assigned us all to start writing a journal. He said it didn't matter what we wrote about; it only mattered that we wrote. I didn't like the idea at all at first, but once I started I couldn't seem to stop. I filled whole notebooks with what I was thinking about. I figured Mom was probably reading them, so I started writing stuff that wasn't true but that I thought she would like. I wrote about hoping to go out with different boys and things, all of which was fiction. For the first four months of school, I didn't go out with anybody other than those meaningless double dates with Lori.

I didn't know if my parents had meant it when they said I could never see Shawn again, but ever since they had forbidden us from seeing each other, they seemed content with the situation. For whatever reason, my feelings for Shawn and the way we acted together stressed them out.

By November, Lori had decided that it was a pain having a boyfriend who lived almost 100 miles away, and she started going out with Chip Lutz. That worked out great, because I was friends with Chip, and Mom and Dad didn't seem to mind when we all hung out together.

After they had been going out a few weeks, Chip had a great idea. He had heard that the Commodores were going to play in Seattle. Because he and Shawn were still really good friends, he had the idea that we could tell Mom and Dad that we were going to see the Commodores. Then we could meet Shawn somewhere in Seattle and all of us go on a double date.

When Chip suggested it, I asked if he had talked to Shawn or not, and if he still wanted to go with me. Chip looked at me like I was crazy. "Are you kidding? He agreed before I even got the words out of my mouth."

Since I hadn't talked to Shawn in three months, I was glad to hear that he still wanted to go with me. I was afraid that, after seeing all the college girls, he didn't want anything more to do with me. The thought of having the chance to spend a whole night with Shawn sounded so wonderful that I couldn't believe it.

This would, of course, mean directly disobeying Mom and Dad. I didn't think it was right that I couldn't see Shawn, and I didn't understand it, but it scared me to think about going against their wishes. Truthfully, I was scared about what would happen if we got caught. When I thought about it that way, though, I knew I had to do it. They had already banned us from seeing each other forever, so they couldn't make that any worse. What else were they going to do to me?

Shawn told Chip that he wanted us to be in Seattle early in the day so we could spend as much time together as possible, but I knew that if we left too early, that would make Mom suspicious and she might not let us go at all. Finally, we agreed that we would leave about 2:00 and get to Shawn's place in Seattle about 4:00.

None of us had much money, and buying the tickets and gas to get there and back took what little we did have, so there was nothing left over to stop and eat on the way. Mom helped out by packing us a lunch that we could eat on the way—tuna fish sandwiches and cookies. We ate them, but by the time we were halfway to Seattle my stomach was so nervous that I wished I hadn't.

Looking back on it now, I don't know what I was so afraid of. Mossyrock was 100 miles away from the concert and it wasn't like Mom had spies all over Seattle. I guess it was a combination of a guilty conscience and an unreasonable fear of getting caught.

The plan was to meet Shawn at his rooming house, but once we got to Seattle and the University District, none of his directions made sense. We got lost in the tangle of one-way streets, and the more lost we got, the more stressed out Chip got. We drove around for a long time just hoping to find any of the streets in the directions, but we were obviously going the wrong way. After about an hour of wandering aimlessly around the fringes of UW, we finally gave up and found a gas station with a payphone.

Chip dialed the number and asked for Shawn. There was a long pause. Chip was starting to dig around for more quarters in case he needed them when he finally said, "Oh, hey. We got lost. We can't find you." After a pause, he said, "We're at a 76 gas station on 45th Ave. We'll just wait here for you, so hurry." Another pause, then: "Yes, of course she's with me."

After he hung up, he turned around looking confident. He flashed a typical Chipper smile and said, "As soon as I told him you were with me, he said he was already halfway here. I think he misses you." That made me feel a little better.

In just a few minutes, Shawn pulled up in a car I didn't recognize. Before it even came to a full stop, he was out the driver's door and hugging me. For just a minute, everything faded away except for the two of us. When he pulled back to look at me, I was a little surprised. It looked like he hadn't had a haircut since I had seen him last. His curly hair was even more out of control than normal. I liked it. I got into the car with Shawn, and Chip and Lori followed in his car.

"Were you expecting the Sin Bin? It's been out of action for a couple of months now, so I've been hoofing it everywhere. This belongs to a friend of mine. I'm sure he won't mind that I borrowed it."

"What? Didn't you ask him?"

"There was no time. He was sleeping. You were standing in the freezing cold at a gas station and I had to come rescue you. He won't mind. He's a friend."

Shawn drove us through a maze of twists and turns. After a few miles, I realized we hadn't even been close to finding him. I wondered how long it had taken him before he could maneuver through all the streets that looked exactly the same. He seemed different, a little more confident, more adult.

He turned down a side street and found a place where we both could park. He pointed up a little hill to a white house crammed in with a bunch of other houses.

"Home sweet home. The guy who owns it is tighter than a miser and doesn't want to pay his own mortgage, so he rents all the rooms out to poor college students like me. I live in a cozy little room in the basement and share the house with six of my new best friends. OK, actually, my room isn't very cozy, but it is in the basement and I do like my roommates. They're good guys."

As soon as Chip and Lori got parked, Shawn led us up a hill and into a side door of the house. He gave us a quick tour of the upstairs, then took me down to his room, leaving Chip and Lori in the living room.

When he opened the door to his room, he said, "I know we don't have much time, but it's important to me that you have a picture in your mind of where I am when I'm writing you letters or just thinking of you, because I do a lot of that."

The room wasn't very big—about the size of my bedroom at home—but it had a bed, a dresser and a desk, and it was clean. On the dresser was the same little record player he had always had, with the 45 of *Always and Forever* playing, just like when we had walked into his house on Damron Road after Prom.

As soon as we were inside, he took me in his arms and pulled me to him. His face was almost touching mine, but he didn't kiss me. He just looked in my eyes and didn't look away. It felt like he was asking me a million questions without saying a word. His blue eyes were serious and maybe a little scared. The confident person that had driven us through the city streets was gone.

"Dawn Adele, I know I haven't seen you in a long time, but I want you to know that nothing has changed. I love you."

"I love you too, Shawn. Just the same."

It was true. As soon as I saw him and was close to him, I knew that nothing had changed. I knew I had missed him more than I had admitted to myself. He smiled and kissed me, long and slow, like he really meant it. I had missed that, too.

We didn't stay downstairs long because Chip and Lori were standing alone in a stranger's house. We collected them from the living room and with Chip driving and Shawn navigating, we made it safely to the Seattle Center Coliseum, where the Brothers Johnson and the Commodores were playing.

It's funny. I had grown up in Southern California, not too far from Los Angeles. After having been in Mossyrock for three years, Seattle felt a little overwhelming with all its tall buildings, non-stop traffic and landmarks like the Space Needle. That feeling didn't dissipate when we walked into the concert. I had never been to a concert before, and the Coliseum was packed to the rafters that night. There were probably thirty times as many people there as lived in the whole town of Mossyrock. Shawn held my hand and acted like he had been there before, so I tried to relax.

There were no assigned seats, but most people seemed to be wandering around on the floor and there were a lot of seats left. I thought we would probably all sit together, but Chip and Lori wanted to try to get right up in front, and Shawn and I didn't want to fight the crowds, so we split up and found a seat toward the back but centered on the stage.

I didn't really know who the Brothers Johnson were, but when they did *Strawberry Letter #23,* I recognized it. It was a strange feeling, watching a band perform a song that I had heard hundreds of times on the radio. That feeling was intensified when Lionel Ritchie and the Commodores came on stage. Shawn and I had danced to a lot of Commodores songs at Hollywood Hollywood, and it was so strange to actually see them singing *Easy* or *Three Times a Lady.*

I really loved the concert and the music, but the longer it went on, the worse the knot in my stomach got. I hadn't seen Shawn in months, and now I knew that every song put me that much closer to not seeing him again for a long time. I didn't think that I could get away with pulling something like this off very often, and I had no idea if or when we could be together again.

When the Commodores had done their last encore, we ran into Chip and Lori on the floor right in front of our seats. There was a huge push to get out the doors, and we got carried along like driftwood on a high tide. Eventually, we popped outside and saw that it had been snowing the whole time we were inside. There must have been five or six inches piled up everywhere. If you were used to the snow, that probably wasn't enough to be a big deal, but no one in Seattle is used to the snow. Drivers were slipping and sliding everywhere.

Chip looked at us and said, "I don't know if we're going to be able to drive home in this, especially if it keeps up. I think we better call Colleen and see what she wants us to do."

"Hey, if you need a place to crash for the night, I've got a warm room and extra blankets…" Shawn said.

I looked at him like he had lost his mind. "Oh, great idea. Let's just call Mom and tell her that we can't make it home, so we're gonna sleep at Shawn's place. I'm sure she'll be fine with that."

He started to say something, realized he wasn't going to get anywhere and closed his mouth. "Listen," Chip said, "my brother doesn't live too far away. I'm sure it would be OK if we spent the night at his house. But, let's call Colleen first and see what she wants to do."

We found a bank of payphones outside the Coliseum and I placed a collect call home. Mom picked up on the first ring.

"Hi, Mom? Uhmm… we just got out of the concert and it's snowing like crazy…"

"I know. I'm watching the weather report on the news. I knew I shouldn't have let you go up there by yourselves."

"We're fine, Mom. It's just snowing. Chip doesn't think he wants to drive us all the way home in this, though. His brother lives around here and Chip says we can stay with him tonight. What do you want us to do?"

The silence stretched out. I knew she didn't want to tell me to stay in Seattle, but she also didn't want us to get in an accident on the way home.

"That's fine, but call me when you get there, and I'm going to want to talk to Chip's brother to make sure it's all right for you to be there."

When we got back to Chip's car, there was something wrong with one of the front tires. While he and Shawn were checking it out, I started to feel sick. Everyone else was gathered around the front of the car, so I went to the back, leaned over and threw up. I hoped I would feel better after that, but I didn't really. I just spent the rest of the night trying not to breathe on Shawn, so he wouldn't know I had vomited.

We headed for Chip's brother's house in South Seattle. It wasn't very far, but the roads were bad and it took us a long time. Chip was a good driver, though, and eventually we got there safe and sound.

By the time we got inside, it was past midnight and everyone in the house had been asleep for hours. I called Mom collect and she asked to speak with Chip's brother. I put him on the phone and he seemed to be mostly listening, just saying "Yeah," or "OK" a lot. Eventually, he handed the phone back to me.

"OK, you can stay there, but I want you to be up bright and early and check the roads. If they're all right, I want you on your way home first thing in the morning."

I hung up and looked around. The house was mostly dark and Chip, Lori and Shawn were all sitting on the couch, looking a little miserable. I sat down next to Shawn and he put his arm around me.

Chip's brother brought us a blanket, which we spread out over the four of us. Then he went into the kitchen and got a chair and set it right in front of the couch. He sat down in front of us and said, "Your mom said I was to keep an eye on everything, so that's what I'm going to do."

It was so late by then that I think we were all too tired to do anything anyway, and we were all asleep almost immediately. That's how I spent my first night together with Shawn, on a couch, wrapped in a blanket with Lori and Chip. I can't say it was very romantic.

In the morning, the roads had been cleared and we knew we had to get going. Shawn walked with me to the car, but he was going to be heading the opposite direction.

"How are you going to get home?" I asked.

"Well, I don't know for sure, but don't worry about me. We're still in Seattle, kind of, so there's got to be a bus line around here somewhere. Once I find a bus, I can find my way home. I'm not worried about that. I'm worried about when I'll see you again. I don't think I can take being away from you anymore."

"I know. Me too, but what can we do about it?"

"I'm not sure yet, but this has got to stop. I'm going to figure something out."

I tried to smile at him, kissed him and got in Chip's car. We sat three across the front with Chip driving, Lori in the middle and me on the outside. As Chip pulled away and headed for Mossyrock, I watched Shawn in the side mirror. He never moved, and I watched him until he got so small I couldn't see him anymore.

Hold the Line

We got home from Seattle by lunchtime. Chip dropped Lori and me off at the driveway and headed for home. I didn't know if he was in a hurry to get home, or if he just didn't want to face my Mom. When we got in the house, she didn't seem to be suspicious or acting funny, though. She just told us she was glad we had made it home safely, and asked us if we had enjoyed the show.

That went on for a few days until one day she and I were in the kitchen and out of nowhere she said, "I know you and Shawn went to the concert in Seattle together. I almost made another sandwich for you to take with you."

I froze, but I knew that my expression had already given me away more than any signed confession I could ever give her.

"Uhhh…"

"Don't bother saying anything. I just want you to know that you're not as smart as you think you are. Your Dad and I usually know what's going on, so you had best remember that."

I still hadn't spoken a word. I was waiting for the next shoe to drop. I figured the next thing she would say would be, 'And now you're grounded until you're thirty,' or 'We're going to take all your babysitting money until you turn eighteen,' or something else drastic. Instead, she didn't say anything until Dad came inside. "Dawn, tell your dad that you are sorry for lying to him and for seeing Shawn in Seattle behind our backs."

I looked at Dad, who looked a little surprised at this development. I wasn't sure he was as in the loop as Mom was saying he was.

"I'm sorry," I mumbled and hurried out of the room.

I should have figured out right then that there wasn't all that much that they could really do to punish me, but I didn't. Instead, it just confirmed to me what I had already figured. Somehow, some way, Mom knew everything I did and I couldn't ever get away with anything.

It was a mistake going to Seattle to see Shawn. Not because we had gotten caught, since there didn't seem to be any real downside to that, but because it made it a lot harder to go back to school and be unable to talk to him again. I missed him more than ever, but I didn't have anyone to share that with, so I kept it inside.

After riding to school with Shawn the year before, I hadn't been able to stand riding the bus back and forth to school. Luckily, we only lived a mile away from school, so unless it was pouring, I walked both ways.

One afternoon in early December it was cold but clear, so I was walking home like usual. I was in the same miserable frame of mind I was always in when I was alone. When I was around Mom and Dad or my friends, I put on a mask of happiness, but when I was alone, I could let the mask slip off and let my real feelings show—to myself, at least, if to no one else.

When I came to the blinking light where I crossed Highway 12, I saw someone tall and skinny standing in the woods on the other side. It almost looked like Shawn, but I knew he was in Seattle and his car was broken down. When I crossed the road, he stepped out from behind some trees and I saw that it really was him. I felt my heart leap. I ran toward him and hugged him.

"I only have a few minutes, or Mom will know something is going on," I said.

"I know. This won't take long."

He smiled at me and I saw tears in his eyes.

"What's wrong?"

"What's wrong is that you are the most important person in my life and I don't get to see you every day, or ever, really. Being away from you these past few months has been the hardest thing I've ever gone through. Since I saw you at the concert, I've spent every day trying to figure out a way so that no one can ever separate us again."

He reached into his pocket and took out a small blue box. He pulled it open and I saw two rings inside. They were yellow gold with a small diamond. There was a pattern in the rings so that they fit perfectly together, like a single ring.

"Dawn Adele, I feel like I can't live without you. I know I can't be happy. Will you marry me?"

I was so torn. All I wanted in life was to be with Shawn. When we were together, I was happy. I always felt safe with him. I felt things I had never felt with anyone else. But as much as I wanted it, I couldn't see any way for it to happen. Mom stood like a roadblock between us and our togetherness. When I thought of marrying Shawn, all I could think of was "Yes," but all I could feel was a sense of dread. In the end, everything I felt when we were together won out.

"Yes, Shawn. I will marry you, but how?"

"I have a way, but it will take a lot of risk on both our sides. If you're willing to do it, so am I, but if you're not, we can just wait. You'll be fifteen in just a couple of weeks. Right after that, I can come pick you up. We can go get on a plane and fly to Mississippi. Once we get there, we can get married. It's the only state where you can get married at fifteen without a parent's permission."

"Can you really get us plane tickets?"

He nodded. "Terri told me that she'll loan me the money for the plane tickets and everything else we'll need. We can do this."

"OK. I'll do it. When?"

"I don't know yet. I'll get in touch with you after your birthday and let you know. I love you, baby, and this is the only way I know to fix it so that we can always be together."

"I love you, too, but I've got to go, or Mom will know something's up."

"I know."

"I can't keep these," I said. Taking those rings off my finger was one of the hardest things I had ever done. They looked so right on my hand, but I took them off and gave them back to Shawn. I kissed him, turned around and headed for Damron Road.

My head was spinning. Every step I took away from Shawn, the more unreal it became. By the time I got to my front yard, it almost felt like it hadn't happened at all.

When I opened the door, Mom was standing just inside, waiting for me, which she never did.

"What's this about a ring?"

Oh, my God. I would never know what combination of

witchcraft and intuition she used to make these incredible leaps, but so often they were right. Did the woman have me under twenty-four-hour professional surveillance? Again I froze, and knew that I had given myself away.

"Shawn was waiting for me when I walked home. He asked me to marry him."

She nodded and frowned, like that was just the answer she had been expecting.

"And what did you say?"

"I told him 'no,'" I lied. I was hoping that by confessing the worst of it—that Shawn had been there and asked me to run away with him—that I could hide the most important thing; that I intended to do it if I could find a way.

She turned away and didn't say anything else for a while, but I could see the wheels turning. The fact that she had somehow known what was happening when there was no way she could have known scared the crap out of me. How could we ever hope to run away together if she knew all our plans before we did?

A few days later, she told me that she had talked to my brother Brian who was a cop in Los Angeles, and that he had told her how smart I was to have told Shawn 'no.'

"Brian said that if you two had crossed state lines and you even had your shoes off, he could be charged with a felony. Believe me, that's exactly what we would have done. Instead of being married, he would have been spending a long time in prison. I really have no idea what he's thinking."

I knew he was thinking that he loved me and that we just wanted to be together, but I didn't say that. Even then, it was hard for me to figure out why they wanted so badly to keep us apart. Shawn and I didn't smoke, didn't drink, didn't do drugs, and we weren't having sex. We ran off to Doss Cemetery and got naked together every chance we could, but even that was innocent compared to what some of the girls told me they did.

From the moment I told Mom that Shawn had asked me to marry him, something changed. Even during the time we had been separated, she hadn't really said anything bad about him, just that she thought we shouldn't be spending so much time together. Now, every chance she got, she said that she thought that Shawn was using me, and I had been nothing but his puppet. Looking back on it, I wonder what exactly he was supposedly getting out of me being his puppet, but at the time I didn't think to question my mom.

A few days before Christmas vacation started, Lori and I walked home from school together. As soon as we got in the house, Mom and Dad were waiting for us. Mom said she wanted to talk to us. I wondered what new secret of mine she had dug up and wanted to confront me about.

"We know how hard it has been for you to be separated from Shawn. We are both proud of you that, other than the trip to Seattle, you have stuck to what we asked you to do and stayed away from each other. Also, when Shawn had the silly idea about asking you to marry him, you were mature enough to know that was a bad idea. So, we've decided to give you two one last chance to see each other."

I couldn't believe it. I had wanted her to say that for so long that I had given up on it ever happening. I waited for the "But…" to come, and it did.

"But this time around, there are going to be a lot more rules. For one thing, we don't want to see or talk to Shawn. He is not welcome at this house or on our property. You two are not to see each other too much, or even every day. Also, you have shown you can't be trusted, so you won't be allowed to be alone together. You'll have to have a chaperone of some kind with you at all times. Finally, you will always have a set time to be home. If you miss any of those times by even a single minute, this will all be off and you will be permanently banned from each other."

That actually sounded pretty good to me. I mean, we were already permanently banned from each other, so no matter what, we wouldn't be any worse off.

"OK," I said, trying to keep any excitement out of my voice. "When does this start?"

Mom looked a little surprised. "Now," she said.

"Can I call Shawn and tell him?"

"Make it quick."

I was just happy that she hadn't thought to ask me how I had Shawn's number in Seattle memorized when I supposedly hadn't talked to him months. Even Mom missed a cue now and then. I called Shawn, but because he lived in that rooming house, he never answered the phone. A man answered. When I asked for Shawn, he said, "Well, he's really not supposed to get calls at this number, but I'll see if he's in his room." I heard the phone on his end clunk down and I started watching the second hand of the clock in the living room sweeping around, ticking off my time.

I was beginning to think I was going to have to hang up without talking to him when I heard his voice on the other end of the line.

"Hello?"

"Shawn, it's me."

"Oh my God. Hi, baby. Is everything OK?"

"We can see each other again!" My control had slipped for just a second and I had let my excitement shine through. I looked at Mom. It felt like her eyes were boring into me.

"What? Seriously? How did that happen? And why?"

"I don't know for sure, but we can. Mom just told me. But, she says it has to be different this time. We've got a lot more rules and if we don't follow them one hundred percent, we won't be allowed to see each other anymore."

"That is so unbelievable! That means that we don't have to run away to be together…"

I interrupted him by saying "Yeah. OK, I've gotta go. I can't stay on the phone."

He got the clue. "Oh. OK, baby, I get it. Can I drive down and see you tomorrow?"

"Yeah, but one of the rules is that you can't come to the house. Just call me when you get here and I'll meet you in the yard."

"Weird, but OK, whatever, baby. I can't wait to see you!"

I saw Mom look pointedly at the clock. "Gotta go. See you tomorrow."

I hung up the phone and tried to process everything that had just happened. I couldn't, so I just went to my room, wrote in my journal, listened to music, and waited for tomorrow to arrive.

I spent most of the next day hanging out at my window, watching for Shawn. I was expecting him to be driving the Vega, but instead, he showed up in a little brown car.

I walked as casually as I could out to the living room and said, "Shawn just got home. I'm going to go say hi."

"That's fine," Mom said. "Just remember the rules."

"I know. I know."

I closed the front door quietly and then ran as fast I could across the yard. Shawn was standing beside the car smiling, holding his arms open for me. I slammed into him and pushed him back against the door of the car. He laughed and said, "Hey, I'm glad to see you too," then he pulled me and held me close. We were both aware that there might be eyes on us though, and we didn't want to blow things before we even got started, so we just held hands and stared at each other.

"So, I can't go to your house. Can you come over to mine?"

"Depends. Is your Mom in the house?"

He looked over his shoulder, checking to see if her car was in the driveway. "I think so. Let's go find out."

We walked across his yard and into his house. It all felt so familiar, but also so strange. Shawn poked his head through the sliding glass door and called, "Mom? Are you here?"

She came around the corner from the kitchen. She always seemed to be in the kitchen. "Hi, honey. Hello, Dawn. Haven't seen too much of you around here lately."

We walked inside and Shawn took my coat. We sat down on the same floral couch we had laid on during Prom night. Other than the Commodores concert, we hadn't talked to each other in almost six months. For once, communication between us didn't flow easily.

After just staring and smiling for a couple of minutes, a serious look crossed Shawn's face.

"I just don't get it," he said. "What changed their minds? I thought they were pretty happy with the status quo."

"I don't know for sure, but I think maybe your dad came over and talked to Mom and Dad."

"Really? What could Dad have said that would have changed their minds?"

I lowered my voice so his Mom couldn't hear in the kitchen. "I think he told them that if they didn't let us see each other, we were going to do something crazy like run away together."

Shawn processed that and said, "I have no idea how he would have known that. I never told anyone other than Terri what we were planning on doing and I know she wouldn't have told him."

I told him the story of how Mom had known about the ring the minute I walked in the door, even though there was no way she should have known.

He shrugged his shoulders. "I guess sometimes they just know stuff."

"I can't stay long. I want to make sure we can keep seeing each other, and I think Mom's got us on a clock."

Shawn sighed and nodded. He knew it was the truth, but I could see he didn't like it. "Can I see you tonight?"

"Probably not. I'm babysitting."

"For who?"

"Sam and Karen."

"Garner?"

I nodded. The Garners lived in the house right next door to Shawn's parents. I could already see what he was thinking. "You can't come over. We're not allowed to be alone together. That's one of the rules."

"I know. Don't worry. I won't do anything to blow it for us."

He walked me to the front door and out onto his porch. I turned to give him a quick kiss good-bye. When I did, he whispered in my ear.

"See you tonight."

Tonight's the Night

Mom was happy to see me back so soon. "Well, that was quick. Are you going to see each other later?"

"No, I'm babysitting for the Garners tonight, remember? I think Shawn's going to a movie or something. It was just nice to be able to see him."

I wasn't sure what I wanted. I knew I wanted to see Shawn, and I definitely wanted to spend some time alone with him, but I was scared we would get caught if he came over. The Garners' house had a big window that opened out to the road, and you could see right into their living room if you drove by the house. I decided to just take it as it came. If he came over, I could always send him away. Or so I tried to tell myself.

I got to the Garners' house a little after dinner. When they left, they said they would be home late, but that I should put their little girl to bed by 8:30. By 9:00, the house was quiet except for the television. I was watching *Let's Scare Jessica to Death,* which seemed like a great idea right up to the moment that Jessica had found a body floating in the lake. Then I wished I had found a *Gilligan's Island* rerun or something. I heard a rhythmic tapping coming from the back of the house, so I got a butcher knife from the kitchen and went to see what was causing it. Of course, it wasn't the boogeyman. It was just Shawn, knocking gently on the back door.

When I let him in, he had that wide-eyed *Did I do something wrong?* look. He knew I could never be unhappy with him when he had that goofy look on his face. I opened the door to let him into the hallway but whispered, "You can't go into the living room. What if Mom and Dad drive by and see you?"

"I have thought of everything," he said. "C'mon." He

dropped down onto his hands and knees and crawled down the hall, stopping to look over his shoulder and smile. I followed behind, wondering what kind of a man-child I was in love with.

When he got to the living room he sat down on the floor with his back to the couch and patted the floor beside him. "See? They can't see." He was always his own best audience for his jokes, but I sat down close beside him and rested my head on his shoulder. We started out watching the movie, but eventually we figured out that no one was really trying to scare Jessica to death and that it was just a cool-sounding title. Then I realized that I was sitting really close to the person I loved, that I hadn't seen him in a long time, and that we were basically alone together in the house.

I haven't mentioned it yet, but during all the time we were dating, Shawn wore Jovan Musk cologne. Of course, he had put it on tonight and it had mixed with his own scent to make me forget about being afraid of getting caught by Mom and Dad, at least for a few minutes. The summer before, we had talked about sex a lot. We had decided that we definitely wanted to wait, agreeing that it would be the smartest and best idea. That was also before we had been separated and thought we were never going to see each other again. The logical thing would have been to just appreciate the second chance we had been given. We weren't feeling very logical.

I felt a heat rising in me and lay down on the carpet next to the couch, pulling Shawn onto me. Just when I thought we had gone too far to turn back, I got scared.

"Shawn. Stop."

I honestly didn't think he would be able to stop, but he did. "What's wrong? Are you OK?"

"No, I'm not."

"OK. Come here, baby."

He moved off to the side and pulled me close, hugging me tight. "You're right. I'm glad you stopped us. I wasn't thinking."

"I know, I wasn't either. I want to, but…"

"I want to too, baby, but we know it's not right. Let's just finish watching the movie. We'll be OK."

We rearranged our messed-up clothes and sat again with our backs against the couch, Shawn still safely hidden from view. I rested my head against him again and was glad we hadn't gone too far. It was so nice to just be near him and feel him hold me. I didn't want to lose that again.

When the movie ended, he kissed me, softly and without the heat and pent-up emotion of before.

"I love you, Dawn Adele. I will do anything for you. For now, what I'm going to do is sneak back across the yard and go to bed. I hope I can see you tomorrow."

And we did see each other the next day, and the next. We never found ourselves completely alone like that, which was probably a good thing. Still, even though it had scared me and I had stopped everything, I liked what we were feeling laying on the floor that night.

Over the days leading up to Christmas, we hung out in a lot of different ways. Sometimes I just walked next door and sat in Shawn's living room and played games. His family had bought an Atari video game system, and we were able to kill large chunks of time racing cars or having tank battles. The graphics were so bad that it was kind of hard to tell the tanks from the race cars, but we didn't know any better, so we didn't care.

Shawn had brought a new album with him too—Billy Joel's *52nd Street*—and we listened to it over and over. There was one song on it called *Until the Night* that Shawn loved so much that every time it came on, he would stop whatever else he was doing and try to get me to slow-dance with him to it. I was too embarrassed to dance in front of his mom, but she mostly ignored us while she puttered around the house, and Shawn didn't care.

On Christmas Eve morning, Mom said that Lori and Shawn and I could go somewhere if we wanted. I'm pretty sure she just wanted Lori and me out of her hair, but we were happy to go. I called Shawn and asked him where he wanted to go. Since we were all broke, he suggested we go to the bowling alley in town, Mossyrock Lanes.

Just a few minutes later, I heard him start the car to defrost it. Lori wasn't quite ready to go yet, so I said, "Meet you out there," and ran outside. It hadn't snowed the night before, but it was so cold that the grass crunched under my feet. The car windows were so frozen I couldn't even see Shawn sitting inside.

When I opened the passenger door, the ice cracked and it made a loud noise that scared me and made Shawn laugh. The car's interior felt like a frozen fishbowl.

"Where's Lori?"

"She's still putting the last half a can of hairspray on. She wanted to make sure there was no chance her hair would get messed up in case we ran into a hurricane."

"Good. Then we've got a second. I want to give you something."

He reached in his pocket. For the second time in less than a month, I watched him pull a jewelry box out of his pocket. My stomach lurched. Was he about to propose again?

He smiled happily at me and opened the little box. Inside was a necklace. It had a smooth dark stone that hung off a silver chain. I felt relief flood through me.

Shawn was watching my expression and concern flashed in his eyes. "Don't you like it?"

"Oh, I love it. Thank you."

I didn't want to blurt, 'I thought you were going to propose again, and it scared the bejesus out of me.' That might ruin the moment. Instead, I smiled and kissed him and all was right with the world.

A few minutes later, Lori came out and we drove to the bowling alley. When we got there, Lori said, "I'm gonna go inside and leave you two lovebirds alone out here. Don't tell your Mom!" There were times I really loved that girl.

Going parking in front of the bowling alley wasn't as romantic as being in our spot up at Doss Cemetery but we did what we could with what we had. After we had been making out for a few minutes, I pulled away and said, "I want to talk to you."

"OK, I kind of liked this other thing we were doing, but go ahead. Shoot."

"The other night, when I was babysitting and you came over..."

"Yeah?"

"What if I had gotten pregnant that night?"

The strangest expression came over his face. It was like there were so many thoughts running through his head at the same time he couldn't separate them. I thought I saw fear and uncertainty, and I don't know what all else. "Babe, you couldn't have gotten pregnant. We didn't do anything. We stopped."

"I know, but what if we hadn't stopped?"

"Well, right now you're in high school, I'm a freshman in college and your parents would kill us, so that would be bad. But, in a little while, when we're both a little older, then it would be the best."

I nodded. I heard his words, but I had also seen the fear in his expression and I couldn't help but wonder. We went inside and played air hockey and pinball and didn't talk about it anymore that day.

That night, the three of us walked up town to the Mossyrock Community Church to listen to a Christmas cantata. I really don't remember why we walked that night instead of driving. Maybe Shawn was running low on gas. The cantata was nice, and when we walked out of the church, it was like what had happened the night of the Commodores concert all over again. It had snowed the whole time we were inside and the ground was already covered. It didn't really snow all that much in Mossyrock, so the idea of a white Christmas made us happy.

It kept snowing on us as we walked home. Several people stopped and asked us if we wanted a ride, but it was so nice walking in the snow that we told them no thanks. By the time we got to Damron Road, my rabbit fur coat had turned completely white.

When we got closer to home, Shawn took my hand and stopped me in the middle of the road. Lori kept on walking, so for a minute it was like we were all alone in the middle of a snow globe.

"I love you, Dawn Adele."

"I love you too, Patrick Shawn."

He kissed me so gently on my frozen lips that I wanted the kiss to last forever. Eventually, we realized our ears and cheeks were freezing, and we caught up to Lori before she made it to our house.

Everything was so perfect. I know I should have just let things be and enjoyed the moment, but I wasn't capable of that. Things were weighing on my mind. Shawn was sweet and patient. He agreed with me about waiting for sex, but I also knew he was in college. College girls didn't have an 11:00 curfew and didn't worry about 'going all the way.' What if Shawn met some girl at the University was willing to do what I wouldn't? Would I lose him? The more I thought about that, the more I thought about Shawn and me together on the floor when I was babysitting. I wished that we had gone ahead and done it. I felt a little foolish now, since we had been so close and I had gotten scared and stopped him.

I didn't expect Shawn to push the issue again, especially after our conversation about me getting pregnant at the bowling alley. I knew if it was going to happen, it was going to be up to me.

Later that week, I got a call from another couple in Mossyrock I babysat for. They wanted me to watch their two kids on New Year's Eve. Shawn and I had been planning on going somewhere that night, but we hadn't finalized anything yet. A new plan was forming in my mind. I told them I would be glad to babysit.

I had been right. Our close call at the Garners' had scared Shawn off a little bit. We hadn't even been close to really being alone since that night, and he seemed completely good with just hanging out and talking. I couldn't help but think what would happen after he went back to college, though.

On New Year's Eve, we hung out during the day and played Atari and listened to music.

"So, since I'm babysitting tonight and leaving you all alone, what are you going to do to celebrate the New Year?" I asked him.

"Oh, I've got some pretty big plans," he replied. "I'm thinking of organizing my comic book collection, and then maybe eating dinner with Mom and Dad."

"I don't care what the kids at school say about you. You are a party animal."

He growled at me like Gene Simmons. I suppose I asked for that one.

"Sorry that we can't be together."

"You know," he said, "I was planning on spending the entire Christmas break in Seattle, by myself in that little basement room. Instead, I've been down here with you. There is nothing for either of us to be sorry about."

"You are a good boyfriend."

"Correction. I am the best boyfriend."

I sighed and shook my head in mock despair. "I love you, Patrick Shawn."

"Always and forever, Dawn Adele."

I went home and put a little more effort into getting ready

than I usually did for a babysitting job. I wanted to look good for tonight.

Late in the afternoon, Mom and Dad went into Mossyrock. Now was my chance. I grabbed the phone and dialed Shawn's number, listening all the time for the distinct click of someone else on the party line eavesdropping.

Of course, it was Shawn's mom who answered. "Oh, hi. Is Shawn there?" I said.

I knew he was. I could look out the window and see his car. "Sure, he's just in the living room. I'll get him for you."

I heard her set the phone down and say, "Shawn. Dawn."

Almost immediately, I heard "Hellooo?" in what I'm sure he thought was a suave voice. He just sounded silly, and I wasn't feeling silly at all.

"Are you still a virgin?" I asked.

That took some of the wind out of his sails. "Last time I checked. Why?"

"Not after tonight, and that's a promise."

"What? Why? How come?"

"Do you really want to ask, or do you want to just come see me?"

I heard silence for a few seconds. "Where?"

I gave him the address of the house where I was babysitting. "I'll put the kids to bed at nine. Come by about ten and I'll be waiting."

"If you're sure, I'll be there."

"I'm sure. See you at ten."

I put the phone down and finally let myself breathe again. I had wanted to sound older and mature, but I hadn't felt that way at all. I felt butterflies in my stomach the rest of the day and evening, but it was like the feeling I got when a rollercoaster was slowly climbing up that first big hill.

Everything was normal with the babysitting job. The kids were good and went to bed and sleep without too much of a fuss. By 9:30, I was sitting on the couch watching Dick Clark's *New Year's Rockin' Eve* and wishing I had told Shawn to be there earlier. I hated the waiting. The television was on, but I was watching the street in front of the house more than the show.

A few minutes before 10:00, Shawn pulled up and stopped. He turned his headlights off, but I could see the windshield wipers still going. He sat there so long, I wondered if he was trying to arrive at exactly 10:00. I couldn't help but wonder what he was thinking and feeling.

If he had been a regular boy, it would have been, 'I'm about to get lucky!' or something even more crude, but Shawn wasn't like that. I wondered if maybe he thought we were making a mistake, and that was why he wasn't coming in.

Eventually, I saw the dome light come on when he opened the car door. He ran through the rain and up the steps until he was under the cover of the tiny porch. He knocked so quietly that I wouldn't have heard it if I hadn't been standing right at the door.

I opened the door and let him in. He was dripping wet from running the few yards between the car and the house. Since I had started this, it was supposed to be my show, but I wasn't sure what to do anymore. I didn't know if I should just jump up in his arms and start kissing him, or if I should let him take the lead.

That was a big part of the problem. Usually, when we came close to actually sleeping together, we were trying hard not to do that. Tonight, now that I had stated our intentions, we were supposed to do it, but we had no momentum at all.

We sat down on the couch and watched TV for a few minutes. I was getting ready to say, 'Just doing this is kind of nice, isn't it?' when Shawn slid across the couch, put his arm around my shoulder, and pulled me toward him. I didn't want him to think I had brought him here under false pretenses or that I was going to stop again, so I kissed him. He kissed me behind my ear and down my neck. After that, I stopped thinking for a while until I looked down and saw that we had ended up on the floor again.

And that was it. We weren't virgins anymore. No matter what else would ever happen, we would always know that we were each other's first.

Shawn kissed me gently and said, "See, I told you we would be a perfect fit."

This just showed that no matter what the circumstances were, he was going to make a bad joke. I looked at him and saw that he was still wearing a very long, blue turtleneck and his socks. At times, he was the most romantic boy in the world. At other times, he was... this.

We both got dressed and sat a little awkwardly on the couch. I thought back to eight months earlier, when we had been naked together for the first time on his mom's couch. That night, everything had seemed to happen so naturally. This night, everything had felt forced and a little unreal.

After a few minutes he said, "I love you, baby, but I guess I should probably go. It wouldn't be too good for either of us if they came home and found me here."

I nodded and walked him to the door, holding his hand. One more kiss and he was gone. It was still pouring outside. I watched him race to his car again and struggle to get it unlocked. By the time he got inside, he looked like he had just stepped out of a shower. I watched as he sat there again for a long time without moving.

When he finally pulled away, I watched his taillights fade into the distance. I took inventory. I was the same person I had been before. I didn't feel all that different. I wondered what life would be like for us now. Would Shawn want to do this every time we went parking up at Doss Cemetery now? Would we ever be able to go back to lying naked and innocent together, or had we killed that forever?

As Dick Clark counted down the final seconds of 1978 and the ball dropped on Times Square, I wondered where Shawn had gone.

I missed him.

I'm So Afraid

The couple I was babysitting for came home a little before 1:00. I was still awake and sitting on the couch. I called my Dad and we all stood in the living room waiting for him to come pick me up. They made small talk with me, asking if the kids had been any trouble and joking with me that I had probably had more fun watching TV than they had out with their friends. I could tell by the way they were talking that they didn't suspect that Shawn had been there.

When I got home, Mom was still sitting up in the living room, working on a craft project. I mumbled goodnight to her and went straight to my bedroom. I knew I wouldn't be able to sleep for a while, but I changed into my jammers anyway and climbed into bed. After laying in the darkness for a few minutes, with the same thoughts running through my head over and over, I heard a car pull into the side yard.

I pulled back the curtains and watched Shawn get out of his car and go into his house. I had thought he would have been home long before me. I had no idea where he had been.

The walls between the rooms in our house were really thin, and you could hear even a normal conversation through them. I heard Mom and Dad's door shut. I could hear Mom say, "He just got home." Dad mumbled something, and then I heard Mom say, "I just know these things. He was there."

My heart sank. No matter what I did and no matter how careful I was, she just knew things. I would never be able to get away with anything. I wondered what the consequences would be from this. Would she call me on the carpet in the morning and pull it out of me? If I denied it, would she ban Shawn and me from seeing each other again anyway?

Other thoughts swirled around my brain, like a dog chasing its tail. Ever since Shawn had left the house, I couldn't shake the feeling that I already knew I was pregnant. At first, I was able to convince myself that I was just being paranoid and that there was absolutely no way I could already know if I was pregnant or not. The longer I lay in bed without being able to sleep, the more convinced I became that I was. The more I believed it, the more I had to think about what I should do next.

Should I just break down in the morning and tell Mom everything? That would be comforting in some ways, because then she would tell me what I needed to do next. It would also be the end of everything between Shawn and me. She would never let us see each other again.

I considered just staying awake, so I would be up and dressed when I saw that Shawn was up. I could catch him before he left to go back to Seattle in the morning. But if I did, would he even believe me? Or, more likely, would he tell me what everyone knew: that you can't possibly know you're pregnant just a few hours after you have sex?

I thought I was going to end up staying up all night, but just as I saw the sky starting to lighten outside my window I fell asleep. I was so tired, I slept like the dead until late in the morning. As soon as I woke up, I remembered the last thing I had heard Mom say about Shawn coming home right after me and immediately got a nervous stomach. I looked out my window and saw that Shawn's car was gone, so I had missed him.

I walked out into the living room rubbing sleep out of my eyes.

Mom said, "Good morning and almost good afternoon. We thought you were going to sleep the whole year away."

I looked at her a little grumpily out of the corner of my eyes and saw that she was just watching the parade and eating lunch, not paying attention to me at all. I relaxed a little bit. If she knew anything, she would have woken me up hours before. I made a bowl of cereal and saw that the parade was already over. I was sorry I missed it, because I loved watching all the floats and bands. A football game was on and Dad sat down to watch it. It was just another normal day, and I had been worrying myself sick about Mom finding out for nothing. Or, so I told myself.

I put my cereal bowl in the sink and went back to the room I shared with Lori. She was still sleeping, but I woke her up. She acted a little pissed about being woken up at noon, but I told her I wanted to tell her something. She forgot all about being mad and jumped over to my bed.

"Shawn and I had sex last night."

She smiled and nodded a little bit, like she might be expecting something a bit more earth-shattering. "OK. Well, that's good, right? How was it?"

I realized I didn't want to talk to her about it. Too late. "It was fine. I think I might be pregnant."

She actually laughed at me. Lori had been sexually active for a while. Now it felt like she was a lot older than me, with the wisdom of the ages to share.

"I was a little scared my first time too, but don't worry. Even if you were, you wouldn't know about it for months. You've got a guilty conscience. Don't worry, it gets easier. The chances of you getting pregnant on your first time are not good. Unless..." She leaned forward, looking serious. "Does he have Super Sperm?"

I pushed her with both hands and she almost fell off the bed, although she might have done that anyway just from laughing at me so hard. I didn't like Lori making fun of me, but I did have to admit it made me feel a little better.

By the time I got back to school the next day, I was a little less worried. Deep down I still had this strong feeling that I was pregnant, but I just ignored it. That first day back I told my friends Cindi, Devi and Cheryl what happened. They were all still virgins.

When I told them, they were supportive, but I also felt like it put a little distance between us. They all thought it had been a mistake. We had all been 'good girls' and they still were, as society defined girls. I was 'faster' now than they were, and that put me on the outside. Still, it was nice to have them to talk to. I told them I thought I might be pregnant too, and they didn't laugh at me like Lori did, but they didn't have a lot of advice, either.

I never had a chance to talk to Shawn the whole month of January. Mom wouldn't let me make a long distance call, so that was out. Also, the Vega was still broken down, so he couldn't drive home for the weekend. Instead, we wrote letters back and forth, written on real paper, put in real envelopes, stamped and put in mailboxes. It was always a good day when I got home from school and found another letter from Shawn, although sometimes I wondered if maybe Mom had managed to open and re-seal them.

They were pretty typical teenage love letters, I guess. Sometimes we would write out the lyrics to songs and send them, or I would write a poem for him to tell him how I felt. We were able to make plans for the future now, and those plans didn't have to involve running away to Mississippi and getting married. We did try to figure out when we were going to be able to get together and see each other, but that was kind of a slow process through the mail. Eventually, we decided that he would come down and spend the weekend before Valentine's Day in Mossyrock. He was going to drive down after his last class at the UW on Friday, the 9th of February.

On the last day of January, I had volleyball practice and got home after it was already dark. Mom said that Dad and Lori had gone to the store because she wanted to talk to me. That was never very good news, but I just took a deep breath and nodded. When Mom and I had our little one-on-one conversations, I often stood over the back of her chair and leaned over so our heads were close together. I went and stood around behind her and said "OK, what?"

"We know that you and Shawn had intercourse and I know that you are afraid you might be pregnant." Her voice was calm and flat, like she had asked me what kind of potatoes I wanted to go with dinner.

I froze. This was a life-changing moment and I tried to think as fast as I could. Was there anything I could say that would change how this was going to turn out? I couldn't think of anything, so I just said, "Why do you say that?"

"Don't play games. I got a phone call from one of your friends today. They're worried about you, and of course, so am I."

"Who called you?"

"I'm not going to tell you, and it doesn't matter anyway."

I felt scared, lost and more than a little numb. I'd been thinking about this moment for a month. Now that it was here, I still didn't know how to react.

"So then, what have you got planned?"

"I don't have anything planned," I said honestly.

"Let's start with this, then. When is your next period due?"

112

"I don't know. I don't keep track."

"Have you had a period since that night?"

"No." I wanted to add, 'If I had, would I still be so worried?' but I didn't.

"This is what we are going to do, then. We're going to wait a few days. Maybe now that we've talked about things, you'll be able to relax and it might come over the next few days. If that doesn't happen, then we'll go out town next week and get a pregnancy test."

"OK." I was still scared and waiting to find out what was going to happen next, but I have to admit it already felt better to let her be in charge. I'd tried being in charge for the last month, and I hadn't done a very good job.

"Next. I don't think I even need to say this, but obviously this is the last straw for Shawn. We gave you two every chance to follow the rules and you couldn't do it. You two will never see each other again."

I heard her words, but I didn't really feel the impact of them. I was still waiting to see what was coming next.

"Now, let's talk about what we are going to do if you are pregnant. If you are, there are two options. You can keep the baby, or you can have an abortion."

I shrunk away. This was a conversation I knew had to happen, but I wasn't ready.

"If you decide to keep the baby, I will raise it until you are out of school and able to take care of it yourself. Then it will be your responsibility. If you decide to have an abortion, then that's it. It's a small procedure and you'll be able to go on with your life."

"We don't have to decide right now, do we? Can't we wait until we know for sure?"

I had just turned fifteen the month before. I knew I wasn't ready to raise a baby, but I didn't want Mom to raise this baby. I loved her, but as I had gotten older I had started seeing things that Mom did with me that I didn't want done with my baby.

"Of course we can. I just wanted to get everything out in the open so there won't be any more skulking around and keeping secrets. That's not good, and we won't have any more of it. Now, go wash your hands and get ready for dinner. I made homemade macaroni and cheese and I know you like that."

Every day, I hoped and prayed that I would start my period and not have to worry about making this decision, but every day was just like the one before it.

I also hadn't been able to find a way to get in touch with Shawn and let him know what was going on. Mom still wouldn't let me use the phone to call him, and I didn't have any money to use the payphone to call him. I tried to write him a letter and warn him, but after I had filled up my wastebasket with crumpled papers, I had to admit I just didn't know what to say to him.

On Thursday the following week, Mom and Dad kept me out of school and we went out town to Planned Parenthood to get a pregnancy test. I had always heard that it took a long time to get the results back, but they told us that if we wanted to wait, they would let us know.

Dad waited in the truck while Mom and I sat in a little waiting room in total silence. I had a magazine open in my lap, but I wasn't reading it. Mom didn't even pretend to do that, but just kept her eyes straight ahead.

It felt like forever, waiting to hear, but it was less than an hour. Finally a nurse came out and asked me to follow her. We walked down a hallway to a little office and we sat down on either side of an old metal desk.

She opened a folder and looked at me. "I've got the results back. You are pregnant."

I thought I was ready for that, but hearing the finality of those words crushed whatever fantasy I had been maintaining that things were going to be all right. I felt the weight of it crash down on me and I started to cry. I was embarrassed to cry in front of someone I didn't know, but I couldn't stop.

The nurse was ready and handed me two tissues. "I know how hard it can be to find this out, but I can counsel you about what your options are for what happens next if you want."

I shook my head. I tried to talk but had to clear my throat first. "No, thank you. My Mom is outside and she's already talked to me about everything."

The nurse smiled sadly at me. She opened the door and led me back to the waiting room.

As soon as I walked out holding the tissues wadded up tight in my hand and tears still running down my face, Mom knew what the verdict was. She took a deep breath and let it out. She stood up, thanked the nurse, and we got back into the truck with Dad. I saw Mom nod grimly at him.

My entire life had just changed and it wasn't even lunchtime yet. We drove back to Mossyrock, and Mom and Dad dropped me off in front of the high school. I walked through the double doors and into the office. I gave them a note from Mom saying I had been at the doctor.

As I was walking to my locker to get my books for the next class, I ran into a girl I knew a little bit. We were friends, but she wasn't one of my best friends. I don't know why, but I told her I was pregnant.

I didn't tell anyone else the rest of the day, but before the last period was over, every kid in school knew it.

Love Hurts

I should have known better, of course. When I told even my very best friends, one of them had called Mom and told her. So, how surprised should I have been that a girl I wasn't that close to had blabbed the juiciest piece of gossip in all of Mossyrock High School? I probably would have done exactly the same thing.

Besides, Mossyrock had fewer than 500 residents. When someone sneezed on one end of town, someone caught a cold on the other end. When the majority of your town is connected by party lines, secrets are pretty scarce.

That Friday felt surreal. Everywhere I went, I felt like people were whispering about me. Girls who never bothered to talk to me before suddenly did. Boys looked at me differently too. I don't know if it was because they thought I was damaged goods, or if they were hoping I put out now. Through it all, my friends Devi, Cindi, and Cheryl gathered around and helped me through it. I took what comfort I could from them, but it was from a distance too. One of them had called Mom and told her I thought I was pregnant. I asked all of them if it was them and they all denied it. I never did find out who made that fateful call.

I had a volleyball game in Morton that night and I was intent on playing. It was the most normal thing in my life, and normal felt comforting right at that moment.

Normal was not to be. When I walked in from school, the first thing Mom said was, "I need to talk to you."

I wanted to scream. I couldn't even imagine what else could have gone wrong that she needed to talk to me about. My shoulders slumped a little and sat down on the couch.

"What?"

"Now is not the time to take an attitude with me, young lady.

I want to let you know that we've been in contact with Shawn."

My heart leapt a little. I hate to admit it, but I had been so wrapped up in my own misery the past few days, I hadn't even thought about what impact this might be having on him. I wondered what he was thinking, and what he might have to say about our options.

"We had an adult conversation. Everyone stayed calm, but as you can imagine, we are angry with him."

I nodded. *Just get to it, please.*

"This is a hard conversation, and it's one I wish I didn't have to have with you. I would have hoped that you would be older when you learned these hard truths. Although our conversation with Shawn was civil, I was very disappointed in his answers. I was hoping he was more mature than he revealed himself to be. I know this is going to hurt you, but I'm going to be honest and tell you the truth. Shawn was relieved that we are planning on terminating the pregnancy."

That was a lot of bad news to absorb all at once. Shawn wasn't being mature. He didn't want to have anything to do with the baby. The fact that we were "planning on terminating the pregnancy" was news to me. I thought we were still just talking about options and what we were going to do.

"He didn't come right out and say it, but in reading between the lines, I think there are some college girls up there that he is interested in. Having a baby with a high school girl would only slow him down. I'm not very happy about it, but I do think it is probably for the best. When I mentioned the abortion, he immediately offered to pay half of it just to get it taken care of. I'm sorry, honey. I know it's not what you want to hear and we all expected better of him."

I thought I was beyond the ability to be shocked, but I was wrong. I knew Shawn so well and we had shared so much. Even the last letters I had gotten from him were full of love and promises of our future together.

"That doesn't make sense."

"I know it doesn't make sense to you, but that's because you're so young. It does make sense to your father and me. We've thought for quite some time now that he was just manipulating and using you. That's why we've been trying to protect you since last summer."

"I don't get it. Manipulating me for what?"

She sighed and sat quietly for a few moments, like she was debating whether she really wanted to tell me or not.

"Some boys feel better about themselves if they can take a girl's virginity. Once that happens, unfortunately, they kind of lose interest. We think that's what happened here. We're sorry. We tried to protect you."

That was so hard for me to believe. It went against everything I knew to be true. Every time we were in a situation and I asked Shawn to stop or slow down, he always did. He never acted like he was with me just to have sex.

I didn't have anything else to say, so I went into my bedroom and closed everyone else out. I took out my 45 of *Love Hurts* by Nazareth. I set it to repeat and lay down on the bed. I'd held them off in front of Mom, but now I felt the tears come.

It was so hard for me to believe that Shawn had said those things. But, it was my Mom. She was the one person in my life who was always there for me. She was the one who was going to love me and protect me no matter what. Boys might come and boys might go, but moms and daughters are forever.

I examined the idea that Shawn didn't really love me. No matter how I turned it over in my mind, I just couldn't believe that either, but I knew there was no real way for me to know. Time would tell.

Before too long, I had to go into the bathroom and wash my face and get ready to catch the athletic bus to Morton. My head was spinning and I wasn't looking forward to the match anymore, but I knew I had to go. I felt like I'd let myself down. I didn't want to let the team down too.

When we got to the Morton gym, we filed into the locker room and got changed into our uniforms. It turned out we were evenly matched with Morton and we were tied at one match apiece when I glanced over at the bleachers and saw Shawn. This time he wasn't smiling. He was just staring at me. His face was a blank mask.

I said, "Devy. Look." The ball bounced right in front of me. I didn't even move.

Carolyn Sprinkle, who had been queen of the Prom the year before, was now the JV coach. She yelled "Dawn. Welch! Get your head in the game. Let's go."

Getting my head in the game was impossible. All I could think about Shawn. Why was he here? If he didn't want anything to do with me anymore, why had he driven all the way from Seattle? The rest of the game was a blur. I didn't care who won or lost. As soon as the match was over, we gathered our street clothes and headed for the bus still dressed in our game uniforms, just wearing our coats over the top. I had only gotten halfway to the bus when I saw Shawn standing, waiting for me. He reached out his hand.

"Baby..."

I tried to push past him.

"Baby, hold on. How are you?"

How was I? Seriously? I was fifteen, pregnant and abandoned. That's how I was. I shrugged and pushed past him, wondering which of my friends was heading for a payphone right now to tell Mom I was hanging out with Shawn at the volleyball game.

I got on the bus without a backwards glance, but once I was in my seat and hidden by darkness, I looked until I found him. He was standing, rooted in the same spot. He looked so lost and lonely, it pulled at my heart. Then I remembered. I turned my face away from the window until the bus pulled out of the parking lot. Fortunately, the bus was dark enough that no one could see that I was crying again.

By the time I got home I felt completely numb. I walked through the house without speaking to anyone, went to bed and was asleep within minutes. I felt the same when I woke up in the morning. Empty.

When I walked into the living room, I saw that Mom and Dad had rearranged the furniture a little bit. They had taken two of our kitchen chairs and set them at the opposite end of the living room. Mom had also taken her card table out of her craft room and set it up in front of her chair. There were a bunch of papers and notebooks laid out on it.

"Wh...what's going on?"

"Go get dressed. We're going to have a meeting with Shawn and Mr. Bartee from the high school in an hour, and I don't want you looking like you just crawled out of bed."

"Shawn? He's coming here? Why?"

"Never you mind. Just go get dressed and get something to

eat. Then come in and sit down."

My life had become a never-ending carousel of strange events. I couldn't quite get adjusted to one bombshell before the next one blew me off my feet again. Half an hour later I had eaten breakfast and gotten cleaned up. I was sitting on the couch with nothing to do. Mom didn't even want the television on. I walked over to the front door and saw the Vega sitting in its normal spot. I went to my bedroom and looked across the yard at his house, but I couldn't see much of anything. Shawn's stepdad had built a tall cedar fence down the property line when Mom and Dad had banned us from seeing each other the summer before.

I was standing by our woodstove, trying to get my hands to warm up, when I heard a knock on the door. As usual, Mom seemed to be in charge of everything. She looked at me, checked everything in the living room like we were staging a play, and then nodded at Dad to open the door.

Shawn and Mr. Bartee, the English teacher and guidance counselor from school, walked in. Mom asked them to sit down in the chairs at the far end of the living room. I had no idea why Mr. Bartee would be in our house. He and Shawn had been friends when Shawn was still in school, but I didn't think he usually made house calls.

Shawn looked terrible. I hadn't noticed in the darkness of the night before, but he had been letting his hair grow out even more since I had seen him in December. It was long and wild. He was pale and had bags under his eyes. He looked like he was ready to cry. Mom was sitting forward in her chair and her back was very straight. I could tell she was angry, but she was speaking calmly.

"Shawn, thank you for coming today, but this will be the last time you are ever in this house and I hope that is understood. Mr. Bartee, it's very nice of you to give up part of your weekend to come today."

Shawn just looked miserable and didn't say anything, but Mr. Bartee and Mom started talking about psychology and a lot of stuff that I didn't understand at all, so I tuned them out.

I kept watching Shawn. He looked like he had been knocked out and was just sitting up and looking around to see what had hit him. When he first came in, he had been staring at me with a pleading look in his eyes like he was hoping I would get some secret message, but he had given up on that now and he was just staring off into space. I saw that tears had started to run down his face.

Mom said, "I don't know how much Shawn has told you, Mr. Bartee..."

"He's told me enough. I know why we are here."

"Well." Mom paused. "Shawn, you haven't said anything yet. What do you have to say for yourself?"

Shawn jerked a little bit. He started to say something, but stopped, like his throat was too thick to be able to speak. I left the woodstove and walked across the room, ignoring the look I was surely getting from Mom. I went behind Shawn and laid my hand on his shoulder. No matter how he felt about me and no matter how much he may have regretted us sleeping together, I wanted him to know that I still cared for him, still loved him.

When I reached out and touched his shoulder, his head dropped and he broke down completely. The tears that had been leaking out quietly came in a racking sob. He leaned his head back just a little to rest it against my arm. He took a deep breath and held it for a few seconds like he was gathering his strength.

"Colleen, you've told me I can never see Dawn again. I can't agree to that. In three years, she'll be eighteen and she can see whoever she wants."

Mom shrugged and said, "Fine."

I felt his shoulder sag under my hand. He said something else, but it was so quiet I couldn't hear what it was. He stood up, reached into his pocket, and took out a big wad of bills. He laid the money on the table that was set up in front of Mom. "I'd like to be able to say goodbye to Dawn," he said.

Mom shrugged again, dismissively. I got the idea that she didn't care what Shawn did from that point on.

Shawn walked toward me and reached out his hand. He glanced around the room, but there was no place we could have any privacy. He pulled me back over to the woodstove. We stood close together, but Mom was only a few feet away. She was talking to Mr. Bartee again, but I knew she was keeping one eye on us.

Fresh tears were running down his face. I could tell he was having a difficult time talking.

"Dawn Adele, I love you with all my heart. The day you turn eighteen, I will feel exactly the same as I do now. If you still love me then, I'll be here for you."

"Do you remember *I Will Still Love You?*" I asked.

"The song? The one by Stonebolt?"

I had heard that song on the radio a lot lately. It was about love and how it can last forever, even when you are apart. I wanted to tell him that, but now the lump was in my throat and I was crying too. I knew this was the last time I was ever going to see Shawn and I didn't want to let him go. I nodded, but couldn't say anything else.

Shawn leaned down and kissed me gently on the cheek just like he had so many times before. He hugged me to him, but only for a second. Then he looked away.

"Jim? Are you ready to go?"

Those were the last words I heard from Shawn for a long time. Mr. Bartee said goodbye and Mom thanked him again for coming. They walked out the front door and closed it quietly behind them.

Wish You Were Here

Two weeks after Shawn left me for good, Mom and Dad drove me to clinic in Olympia. Sitting in the sterile waiting room, I heard the nurse call my name.

"Dawn? Dawn Welch?

I stood up and looked at Mom. She reached out to try and squeeze my hand, but I pulled it away.

"I'll be right here when you're done."

I nodded and followed the nurse down the long hall. The whole building seemed quiet. My shoes made too much noise as I walked. We turned into a small room with an examining table. The nurse handed me a hospital gown and said, "We'll need you to get changed into this. You can leave your bra on underneath."

Her voice was kind and gentle. If she had said something harsh to me, I think I would have broken down, and I was doing everything I could to not cry today.

I slipped off my shoes and set them in the corner. I got undressed except for my bra and put on the white hospital gown. It tied in the back, but no matter how I arranged it, it never felt like I had it on right. I sat down on the examining table and waited.

Two months ago, as I was turning fifteen, everything in my life had felt good. I had lots of friends and I was with Shawn, my first love. I wasn't the town's hot gossip topic. Now I was sitting on a cold examining table in a poorly-secured hospital gown, waiting for a doctor to perform an abortion I didn't know if I wanted or not. Whether I was unsure or not didn't matter. I felt like I didn't have any choice.

The nurse came back in and handed me a pill and a glass of water. "This will help with your nerves. It will make you feel better."

I was all for that, so I took the pill without asking what it was.

"The doctor will be along in just a couple of minutes." She laid a hand on my shoulder and gave me a gentle smile. "Everything will be all right."

I nodded, but I couldn't help but wonder if anything would ever be all right again.

Comfortably Numb

Now that Shawn was gone, I would have thought he wouldn't be the subject of conversation any more, but I was wrong. Every few days, Mom would bring him up in some new way. The summer before, Shawn had given Mom a ride to the doctor out town because Dad had been working. At the time, she had told me that she was proud of Shawn because he drove like a perfect gentleman and that she would always feel safe with me in the car with him. Now, almost a year later, the story changed. She told me that Shawn had driven "like a maniac" that day and that she had thought he was trying to kill her. I put the discrepancy down to the fact that she had been trying to spare my feelings the year before.

Every time Shawn's name came up, she attached something negative to it. He had used me. I had been his puppet. He had gotten what he wanted and then left me all alone to deal with the consequences. Over time, I came to see Shawn differently than I had before. I realized that when I was with him, I hadn't been able to see things clearly. The love I once felt for him turned sour. I still thought about him, but those thoughts were never good ones. And yet....

No matter what happened, I still felt drawn to Shawn. No matter how many times he was portrayed as the villain, and even after I came to accept that, I could never deny that I felt a pull and attraction to him that would never go away.

The other thing was that I was in mourning, but everyone around me went on with their lives as if nothing had ever happened. Now that Shawn was gone and the abortion was over, it was as if we could all act like it never happened. I couldn't do that. I had lost everything that was important in my life. Losing the baby was the worst part. It was a pain that would never go away. I had also lost the most important person in my life, my Shawn. I didn't know if my heart would ever heal enough from that to really love someone again.

A few months later, I went to my first high school party. For the first time in months, I felt almost normal. I got home late that night, but Mom didn't say anything about it. After that, I got invited to more parties. I pushed my limits pretty fast—I got home a little later and a little drunker after each party. When I did, Mom would say something, but she never did anything about it. She didn't even threaten to ground me anymore. If she had been a little overprotective before, she had gone the other way now and it felt like I could do anything I wanted.

I didn't have anything like a serious boyfriend during that time. After what I had been through, I wasn't ready for that.

The summer between my sophomore and junior years, I met a boy named Lon Miller. He was the same age as Shawn and would have graduated with the class of '79, but he had dropped out of school. When I first met him, he seemed shy and nervous around me. He wasn't the cutest boy in the world, but he did have a few things in his favor. He had a car and he liked to drink. That fit the new lifestyle I had fallen into. I never felt a lot of emotional involvement with Lon, but over time we became a couple. It wasn't even a conscious decision, but I think that after all the intensity and pain of what had happened with Shawn, I wanted to find a relationship where I couldn't be hurt, no matter what.

One night, after we'd been seeing each other just a few months, we got home late from a party. As we pulled into the driveway, I started to get out of the car. We'd both been drinking and I was way past ready to go in and go to bed. When I reached to open the door, Lon leaned across the seat and stopped me.

"I think we should get married."

I sighed. He was so drunk I wasn't sure he would remember asking me the next morning. I was so drunk that I wasn't sure *I* would remember. I had absolutely no intention of ever marrying Lon Miller, but in my slightly addled state, I couldn't find a nice way to say "no."

I was engaged for a second time before my 17th birthday. I

recognized that my life wasn't heading in the right direction.

The odd thing was, even though Lon was the same age as Shawn, and even though he had dropped out of high school and liked to take me to parties and get me drunk, Mom loved him. When I told her I was going to break up with him, she always encouraged me to stick with it and give him another chance. I don't know if she thought that Lon would be easier for her to control or if she could tell I wasn't emotionally invested in him or what, but she never seemed to get tired of him no matter what he did.

At the beginning of my senior year, I couldn't take it anymore and broke up with him. And broke up with him, and broke up with him. He never believed me when I told him I was ending it. Finally, I had enough and I picked a horrible fight with him in the high school parking lot. I threw the engagement ring at him, got out of his car and walked home. By the time I got there, Mom was furious with me. Lon had gotten there first and told on me.

I finally stood my ground with Mom and told her the truth: I had never cared about Lon and by then I was so sick of him I was done with him no matter what.

All during that time, I led a fractured life. At school, I still hung out with the friends I'd had since eighth grade. They didn't go to parties much though, so I ran with a whole different crowd on weekends. I had quit thinking so much about Shawn. We didn't talk. The only reason I ever saw him was when he came home to visit his parents for Christmas or Easter. I knew he had moved on with his life just like Mom had said he wanted to, because every time he came home, he had a different, skanky looking girl with him. I figured he had gotten what he wanted.

A month or so after I broke up with Lon, I started going out with Rick Johnson. He liked to drink and party just like Lon did. Life went on. Mom didn't like Rick as much, but that didn't matter. I wasn't listening to her like I had before. Rick and I stayed together through my senior year and beyond, but it was a hard and violent relationship almost from the start. Life was not getting any better.

After I graduated from Mossyrock High School, I still lived at home with Mom and Dad. I worked at a few different jobs— back at DeGoede's bulb farm, waiting tables at The Wheel Café in Morton, or as a nurse's aide at a nursing home in Centralia. Rick and I still went to parties every weekend, but I had mostly stopped drinking. Rick drank enough that I felt like I needed to be sober enough to take care of him. By Christmas 1981, I had settled into a routine. I worked all week, then sort of partied on the weekends. I wasn't living the life I had dreamed about, but I didn't know how to go about changing it.

The night between Christmas and my eighteenth birthday was a Saturday, which usually meant that we would have gone to a party. It being the day after Christmas, however, nothing was happening. Rick, Mom, Dad and I had been just sitting around the house on Damron Road watching television. Rick had run home for just a minute when the phone rang.

Dad got up out of his chair and said, "Hello?" The funniest look crossed his face. He actually looked scared, and I couldn't figure out who could get that reaction from him. He didn't say a word, but just set the receiver down, turned to me and said, "It's for you. It's Shawn."

My stomach dropped. I couldn't imagine why he would be calling me after three years. What could he possibly want to say? Rick would be back in a minute. If he found me talking to Shawn, there would be hell to pay. My mouth was so dry all of a sudden that I didn't know if I would be able to talk.

"Hello?"

"Dawn? It's Shawn."

I didn't say anything. My mind was a complete blank and I didn't have anything I wanted to say to him.

"I was wondering if you would like to meet me out in the yard for a minute so we could talk. I'm next door at Mom and Dad's."

I couldn't believe it. Was he stupid?

"I don't think so."

"Oh." He said it quietly, like he was surprised. Why would he think I wanted to talk to him now? He had manipulated me, used me and abandoned me at the worst possible time. Now he was surprised that I didn't want to get all bundled up and go bouncing outside to talk to him like we were kids again?

"You don't think so. OK, then. Bye." He said that so quietly that I could barely hear him over the TV.

I hung up without another word, feeling angry and a little

scared—and distant stirrings of the old feelings I had for Shawn.

"What did he want?" Mom demanded.

"He wanted me to go outside and talk to him."

"You said 'no,' I hope. What in the world would you have to say to him after all these years?"

After a moment's pause, she said, "I know what it is. He knows you have a boyfriend now. He knows you're happy and he just wants to stir up trouble for you. He thinks that if he waltzes back in here, it will make you and Rick argue." I didn't say anything, but that explanation made as much sense as any other.

I walked back into my bedroom without turning my light on and looked across the yard at Shawn's parents' house. There were lots of lights on, and I could see people in the living room watching television. Then I saw Shawn step out the door of what used to be his bedroom. He had a backpack over his arm and walked quickly across the snow to a car that was parked right where he used to park the Vega. He got in and started it and sat there waiting for the ice on the windshield to defrost. I guessed he had come down, caused whatever trouble he could, and now he was going back to Seattle and whatever girl he was sleeping with now.

When Rick got back, I told him that Shawn had called. His reaction was pretty much the same as Mom's—that Shawn was jealous that I was happy, and trying to stir up trouble. I was just glad that it didn't lead to a big argument and a fight, like so many other things did with Rick. I also wondered why everyone but me thought I was happy.

After that, I did my best to put Shawn out of my mind permanently. I was mostly successful. Sometimes, if *Stairway to Heaven, Always and Forever*, or one of our other songs came on the radio, it would bring back memories for a minute, but over time it got easier and easier to send them away.

The following summer, things still followed the same routine—work during the week and joyless parties on the weekend. Lather, rinse, repeat, over and over. By then, Rick and I had been together for two years and it was starting to feel long-term. I wasn't head over heels in love with him, but Mom kept telling me that the kind of feelings that Shawn and I had for each other had not been real, that they were just puppy love. She told me that real, mature love was different than that, and that it always took a lot of hard work and sacrifices to make any relationship work. With Rick, it definitely felt like work for me, but I didn't see him making a lot of sacrifices or putting in a lot of effort. Still, over time it was harder and harder to break away from it.

One hot summer day in July of 1982, I had the day off from waitressing at The Wheel. Rick and I were hanging out at my house, not doing much. I heard a knock at the door and answered it. To my great surprise, it was a delivery from Mossyrock Florists. The delivery person handed me a vase with three roses—two red, one white—surrounded by baby's breath.

Rick came over and asked, "Who sent you those?"

"I have no idea."

He narrowed his eyes in disbelief. Rick often thought I was seeing someone else. "Is it someone from your work? A customer? Who?"

"I don't know. I don't see a card."

Without another word, Rick walked out of the house, slammed the door behind him, got in his car, and peeled out down Damron Road. Mom glared at him for rattling her windows but didn't say anything. Mom and I searched the arrangement in vain for a card.

She looked at me and asked "Do you know who sent them?"

Unbelievable. No one believes me.

"No, I really, truly, absolutely, no-doubt-about-it have no idea who sent me this or why."

I thought maybe someone would call and tell me they had sent them, but after a few hours it was as big a mystery as ever. When Rick got back, he was determined to solve it. "Come on," he ordered. "We're going to go find out who sent you those flowers."

We drove to the florists' house and knocked on their door. When they answered, I said, "Hi, you delivered some flowers to me this afternoon, but there wasn't a card with them. Can you tell me who sent them?"

"I remember. I didn't put a card with them because the person who sent them wanted to remain anonymous."

"So, you can't tell us who sent them then?"

"Technically, I really shouldn't. However, if you want to guess, I'll tell you if you are right or wrong."

Mysterious flowers arrive out of nowhere. Rick is so pissed I can see steam coming out of his ears, and this guy wants to play Twenty Questions. "Can you just tell me this? Is it someone local here, from Mossyrock or Morton?"

"They were definitely not from around here, at least not anymore."

As soon as he said that, I knew. "Shawn Inmon." He nodded and smiled an odd little smile.

I looked at Rick. I thought he might be even more pissed, but he actually seemed to relax a little. I guess he thought that flowers from an old boyfriend I didn't talk to anymore were a lot better than having a secret admirer in town.

"It was one of the oddest things I've ever seen," the florist added. "He came strolling into the shop today wearing a cape, an eye patch, and using a cane to walk."

I blinked. I almost laughed, but I held it back.

Rick couldn't help himself. "What? Are you kidding me? That's hilarious. What a freak."

"Is there anything else I can help you with?"

"No, thank you," I said as we walked back to Rick's car. When we got back to Mom's house, I told her what the florist said.

She shook her head, annoyed. "I don't know what we're going to have to do to get him to leave you alone and quit causing trouble for you. He's done enough to hurt you, but it seems like this is becoming a habit with him."

"I know just what to do to take care of it," Rick said. He grabbed the roses out of the vase and walked out the front door.

About ten minutes later, he came back empty-handed. "There. I think that'll do it."

"What did you do?"

"I took the damned flowers back to him and told him that he had done enough to ruin your life already. I told him to quit bothering you by calling or sending you flowers or whatever."

"What did he say?"

"He said he wouldn't bother you anymore."

I didn't see him or talk to him again for more than twenty-five years.

Again
January 5th, 2007

Shawn came through the drive-through again. I was working another double ACS/Bill & Bea's shift.

"Hey, Mom," Connie said. "Your boyfriend's here again."

I almost didn't look, because she was in the habit of saying that to alert me to some ancient, toothless guy, or a customer who had last bathed when Bill Clinton was president. Tonight, though, she pointed to the car idling in the second position in the drive-through. It was Shawn, sitting in a silvery-blue Jaguar. I'm not exactly a car nut, but I recognized the hood ornament.

He had been on my mind a lot since he had appeared out of nowhere. I wasn't mooning over him, for sure, but seeing him had stirred up a lot of memories. He had been the boogeyman in my life for so long that I didn't even bother to question it anymore.

I tended to think of him while driving. Shawn had taught me a few things about driving, like how I shouldn't brake in the middle of a curve or how to change lanes on the freeway without hitting any of the little bumps. Now, I thought of him every time I did exactly the opposite of what he had taught me.

Music had been central to the way Shawn and I had expressed our feelings. The songs we had shared remained so linked to him that they always took me back in time. In fact, when I was alone, I had taken to talking to him when our songs came on. It wasn't sappy 'Oh, I miss you' sort of talk. Instead, when a song like *Baker Street* by Gerry Rafferty came on, I could swear I would hear his voice in my head saying something like, "Do you remember where we were when we heard this song the first time?" My usual response wasn't very romantic or wistful. It would be something like 'get the hell out of my head, you freak.'

Shawn had also shown up in my dreams ever since he'd left me. He was part of a recurring dream, in which we played something like a grownup game of hide 'n seek. Sometimes we were in Mossyrock, sometimes somewhere else, but Shawn was always looking for me, calling me. When I was younger, I hid from him in my dreams because I felt like Mom was looking over my shoulder, about to ground me. Later, the dream had evolved. I dreamed I was hiding from him because I was ashamed of my life and I didn't want him to see me the way I was.

And now, here he was again, driving his beautiful car and wearing a wedding ring in the rundown little drive-in where I was finishing up my second shift for the day. That was great.

When he pulled forward, I opened the window and looked at him.

"You're not going to freak out on me again, are you?" he asked.

A quarter of a century, and he still had not located a filter. I would call it unbelievable, but I'd be kidding myself. It was completely believable that, in all this time, he still hadn't learned not to blurt out the wrong thing.

It pissed me off but good. The last time he had come through, he had said, "We went to school together," as if that was all I had ever been to him—a school friend. Now, here he was again, sitting in a rich man's car and obviously living the good life, making fun of me in that smug, superior way that made me want to throw a ketchup bottle at him. Instead, I dialed my tone down to absolute zero.

"No, I'm over that now." To finish giving him the full picture, I pulled out my order pad, manufactured a wintry smile, and said, "Can I help you?"

He looked like I had slapped him. There had been a little twinkle in his eyes when he first pulled up, like we had been old friends who just hadn't seen each other in a while. Now, he looked like I just stole his puppy.

"Um, OK, I guess I'll have a chicken sandwich and a medium iced tea."

I made a note on my pad, said "I'll get that right out to you," closed the window and walked back toward the grill area. I knew that Shawn was watching me wherever I went, so I made sure that I was extra sweet to all the other customers. I wanted him to know it was just him I didn't like, and not everyone else.

When his order was bagged up and ready to go, I walked back over to the window. I had one hand on the bottom of the bag to balance it. Shawn reached out and cupped my hand with his for just a moment. It was a gesture of familiarity. I pulled my hand away.

"That'll be $8.76, please."

He handed me a ten and said, "It's really good to see you, Dawn."

I made his change and handed it to him. "You too," I said, giving up nothing. I closed the window and turned away.

I'm not sure what I expected from him, but whatever it was, I hadn't gotten it. I guess I wanted him to show me that, at least a long time ago, I had been important to him. Instead, I got "We went to school together" and "You're not gonna freak out on me, are you?"

After twenty-seven years, I thought I deserved more than that from him.

Hold on Tight
January 2009

It was 10:00 on a Monday night, and I was sitting on the couch waiting for the news to show the rest of the week's weather forecast. Life had gotten a little better. Dani, my fifteen-year-old younger daughter, and I were living with a man named Aaron. I had met Aaron a year and a half before, and liked him well enough. From a practical viewpoint, being in a relationship with someone to help share the bills made things more comfortable. I didn't love him, but I hadn't been in love in so long I was pretty sure that part of me was permanently disabled.

I had been able to quit working the second job at Bill & Bea's, but was still working at ACS. We were living in Chehalis and ACS was in Tumwater, twenty miles north. The weather forecast would give me some idea how miserable my commute might be the next morning.

My cell phone rang and I saw it was Connie.

"Hey, what are you up to?"

"Hi. Um, I have to tell you something about Dani."

"What, she's pregnant?" I asked with a laugh.

"Yes."

"What?!?!"

"So you knew already Dani was pregnant? She didn't think you knew."

"No, I didn't know that Dani was pregnant! I was joking. Oh my God."

My hands were shaking as I said, "I've gotta go. I've got to call Dani."

When Dani answered, her voice told me that she had been crying. She had been a rebellious girl all her life, but right at that

moment she sounded small and scared. I was still reeling and had
no idea what to say to her.

"Hi, baby."

"Hi."

"I love you, Dani. We'll get through this. I don't know what
the answer is, or how we'll make it work, but we will."

We didn't talk much longer. There wasn't anything else to
say.

Dani had been a handful from her terrible twos onward.
There was no way she was ready to be responsible and be a mom.
She was just too young. I thought about her boyfriend, Daniel. He
was a sweet boy and I liked him, but even though he was a few
years older than Dani, he wasn't mature enough to be a dad.

Sleep didn't come for a long time that night. My thoughts
kept going in circles, but there didn't seem to be a good solution.
The obvious answer was an abortion. They just weren't ready to
be parents, and I didn't know if I had it in me to raise another
baby while I worked fulltime.

I remembered my own experience and stopped cold. Mom
had told me that she was stopping me from ruining my life, but as
I looked back on it, since that decision everything had gone bad. I
had never had a truly happy time in my adult life.

A few days later I invited Dani and Daniel, plus Connie and
her boyfriend Jamie, over for dinner. Dani and I hadn't talked
much more about the big news. I wanted to have everyone over
for dinner and play a board game, so that we could have a
relaxing evening together. It didn't work out that way.

We were playing Aggravation, and the game lived up to its
name when Connie and Dani got into an argument. I honestly
didn't know what they were arguing about at the time, because
they were sisters and they were always arguing with each other. I
learned to tune it out years ago unless it came to blows.
Unfortunately, this was one of those nights when their arguing
escalated. With so many emotions running just under the surface,
all it took was for one of them to say something minor and the
fight was on. I ended up having to separate them before they
killed each other. By then, all those emotions had boiled out well
above the surface.

"I know you want me to have an abortion," Dani said,
looking at me. "I know you want to talk to me about options, but

it's not going to happen. I'm going to have this baby and there is nothing you can do about it."

That set me back. When I was her age, I had believed everything I had been told, and in the end I did what I was told. When I was fifteen and pregnant, my mom had manipulated me into getting an abortion. Her reasons resembled my own grounds for thinking that an abortion would probably be best for Dani. Yet deep inside, in a place I didn't talk about with anyone, I had regretted it ever since.

My mom raised me to do as I was told, always. It hadn't worked out for me, and for that reason, I raised my girls to question everything—to think for themselves. I achieved that. Here was the living proof, staring defiantly back at me, telling me that she was going to keep her baby.

Nothing else had changed. She was still too young. She would have to change her whole life in order to be a mom to this baby. But that was her decision, not mine, and she had made it. I was proud of her. I hugged her and said, "OK. It's up to you."

"I know it is."

She was still defiant, but I knew the decision had been made. There would be no more talk about options.

After the Love has Gone

Almost five months later, things were moving along. I still wasn't happy about Dani's pregnancy, but I was proud of the way she was preparing for motherhood. She was settling down, focusing on things like school and preparing to be a mom, instead of hanging out with her friends and partying. Although I was mad at Daniel when I found out Dani was pregnant, I was proud of him too. He had a full-time job and he worked hard. He called me and tearfully promised me that he would always take care of 'his family.'

Earlier that week, Aaron had gone to Hawaii on vacation with some friends. I'm sure I should have been upset that my live-in boyfriend went to Hawaii without me, but I wasn't. It was nice having a break from him. That should have clued me in to the fact that I was happier with him gone than with him there.

About mid-afternoon, around the middle of my shift at ACS one day, Connie called my cell phone. She knew I was at work, where I tried not to take many personal calls, so my heart lurched a little. Things were just settling down, and I prayed it wasn't bad news.

"Hi. I'm at work."

"I know, but I think you want to know about this. The people who own Bill & Bea's were checking around on the Internet to see if there were any reviews anywhere. You will never believe what they found. Do you remember when that guy came through the drive-through a few years ago and you freaked out a little bit?"

"Yeah. Why?"

"He wrote a story about it, and I think you're going to want to read it. He says he's still in love with you."

"How do I find it?"

"Just Google "Bill & Bea's" and look for a website called Writing Raw. Click the link and it will take you right to it."

"Crap. We don't have access to anything but email at our workstations. Too many agents were checking their Facebook status and not working, so they disabled it."

"Well, maybe you can check it on the computer when you get home. Just thought you'd want to know that there's some weird dude running around out there that thinks he's in love with you. Bye!"

I could do that, of course. I could finish my work like a good little worker bee, take a leisurely drive home, have dinner and sit down to read what my first love had written about me. Whatever. Patience was never my strong suit.

I went to Jake, one of the Operations Managers at ACS. "Can I borrow your computer for a minute?"

"What's wrong with your computer?"

"Nothing's wrong with it. It just can't access the site I need."

"What do you need to get online for in the middle of a shift?"

"I know it sounds weird, but someone wrote a story about me and I want to read it."

This seemed to amuse him. He smiled and gestured toward his computer. "Help yourself. I'll go get a cup of coffee and then I'll be back. Print it out if you want."

I sat down at his computer, went to Google, and typed in "Bill & Bea's." Sure enough, one of the first results that came back was from a website called WritingRaw.com. When I clicked on the link, it took me directly to a story titled *December, 2006*, by Shawn Inmon.

The first line of the story read, "It had already been a very long day, but I wasn't in any hurry to get home to Enumclaw." I hit 'print' and it started to roll off Jake's printer. I thought it might be just one or two pages long, but paper kept coming. When I pulled the last sheet out of the printer, I saw that the last line of the story was, "My body was in 2006, but my mind, spirit and heart were firmly lodged in the 1970's."

I closed out the window just as Jake came back. He was still smiling a little and looking amused. "Find what you need?"

"Yes, thank you." I hurried back to my own workstation and

sat down to read.

It was basically the story like I remembered it, but I thought he had made himself look a lot smoother than he actually had been. Then I saw that he wrote that he loved me, and that he had always loved me. I *didn't* believe that. I guessed Shawn was finally getting around to fulfilling his dream of being a writer. He was probably stuck for an idea, so he took something that really happened—running into an old girlfriend—and wrote a fictionalized story around that. He had even changed his own name. He called himself "Scott Mitchell" in the story, but he left my name in, which ticked me off.

At the same time, the things he wrote in the story were what I would have loved to have heard from him when he came through my drive-through. I would have liked to have known that I had been important to him once, even if it was a long time ago. Instead, he had said, "We went to school together" and "You're not gonna freak out on me again, are you?" It felt like he was using me all over again, using what we had left of our relationship to write a fictional story. That just figured.

In the back of my head, there was a small voice telling me that it might be real. What if he *had* loved me all this time and I never knew about it? That was a bigger idea than I could deal with.

I found a manila envelope and stuck the story inside it. I did my best to focus on work over the next few hours, but my mind kept wandering back to the story.

When I got home, I immediately went to the desktop computer and signed into Classmates.com. I had signed up for it the year before, but had never gone back. I thought that might be a good place to try and find out about Shawn, and what he had been up to for the last thirty years.

When I signed in, a little icon said I had a new message waiting. When I looked at the date I had received it, I saw that it wasn't new. The date it had been sent was February 23rd, 2008— almost a year and a half ago. It was a note from Shawn Inmon, and it had been sitting in my Classmates account all that time.

Dawn,
I'm sure it seems a little out of the blue to get an email from me, but I would like to have a chance to talk with you. I'd like to

see if we could be friends. When I left you in 1979, I was counting the days until I could talk to you again, and now over 10,000 days have passed and we haven't had a single conversation. That seems wrong to me.

I don't have any way of knowing where you are in your life right now, but I'd like to catch up with you. It's possible you're happy with not having spoken to me for the last thirty years. I wasn't sure if your first reaction at seeing me again was happiness, horror, or just shock, but I admit it was a little deflating when you looked at me and said "Shawn who?" I would like to get to know you again, but if you don't have an interest in that, just drop me a line and let me know and that'll be that. I agreed not to see you until you were 18 all those years ago because I thought that was what was best for you. My regret now is that I didn't talk to you about that decision. That was wrong, and I'm sorry.

I hope to hear from you…

Shawn

I read it over three more times, trying to capture the flavor of what he was saying. More than a year after I last saw him at Bill & Bea's, Shawn had sent me a letter the only way he could. He sounded contrite and apologetic, unlike when I had seen him last. He didn't sound much like any of my mental images of him.

I didn't know what to do. I hadn't thought about Shawn in a long time; now I couldn't get him out of my mind. I hadn't thought of any of the happy memories of Shawn in decades. That had been a weakness I couldn't afford if I wanted to survive. Besides, first Mom, and then for many years Rick, had told me that what Shawn and I had when we were young was nothing but a fantasy. They told me that the fantasy had ruined me for a real-life love.

For the first time in thirty years, I closed my eyes and let the memories come. I remembered a skinny young boy riding his bicycle around the neighborhood or playing in his yard, the hours that we talked and played together in our side yard, and the way he always seemed to be there to help me when I needed it. Then I thought about our best times, the gentle kisses, the laughter, the safety I found in his arms. None of those memories matched up very well with the boogeyman image I carried around all these years.

Even so, I remained wary, and for good reason. I had trusted too many times in my life, and not once had it turned out well in the end. Why would this be any different?

I almost couldn't believe I was doing it, but I sat down at the computer and started writing an email to send to the address he had left me on Classmates.com.

Well, hello.

I don't know if I am fated to contact you or what. I logged into Classmates.com and saw the message you sent how long ago? I haven't been there since I signed up over a year ago. Then Connie, the daughter you met, called me to let me know some odd dude wrote a story about me and you can find it if you Google Bill & Bea's. I was mortified. My daughter now knows that "my first" is still in love with me.

I'm happy, in love, and my two daughters are happy. I am a supervisor for Verizon Wireless customer service, which means I get called terrible names all day, every day. The only difference between that and my marriage is that now I get paid for it.

Sorry I didn't recognize you at Bill and Bea's. I was what, 15 when I saw you last? I don't remember a lot of that time. In your message you asked if we can we be friends. Well, there's no such thing as too many friends. However, my daughter thinks you are odd. I wonder myself.

Dawn

It might have sounded a little defensive and angry, but that was how I felt. Well, part of it wasn't completely honest—I wasn't all that happy or in love—but he didn't need to know that. I still had no idea how much I could trust him.

I stared at the screen for the longest time, took a deep breath and hit "send."

It was a little after 10:00, so I turned on the ten o'clock news to see if it was supposed to be as warm the next day as it had been today. The forecast showed nothing but blue skies and sunshine ahead.

"I'll believe it when I see it," I mumbled to myself, and went to bed, happily alone.

Because the Night

As soon as I woke up the next morning, I turned the computer on and checked my email account. Nothing. I already regretted sending the message. I went to Google to see if there was a way to pull back a sent email if the recipient hadn't read it, but apparently you can't do that.

I got dressed and had my usual healthy breakfast—strong coffee with hazelnut creamer—and headed off to ACS. When I got there, I checked my email again. Still nothing, so I did my best to forget about the whole thing. It had been dumb to send him anything. He had published that story months ago and written that email a year and a half before. He had probably forgotten the whole thing and moved on to someone else.

In mid-morning, I logged into my email and there it was. There was no subject, but the sender was Shawn Inmon. I felt butterflies, which was silly. This was the boy/man I had despised for three decades. Why should I care what he thought? I clicked on the email.

Hello Dawn,

First, let me apologize for the fact that your daughter stumbled across that story online. I thought I had changed enough information so it wouldn't pop up on a Google search. Obviously, I was wrong. I really am sorry. It was never my intent for anyone you know to see it and embarrass you.

I contacted the site where the chapters were posted to have them taken down. They're already gone, so nobody will accidentally run across them again. Anyway, please accept my apology for any embarrassment I may have caused you.

In your email, you said you were in love, and I'm glad for you. When I knew you thirty years ago, I thought you were the best person I had ever met. You deserve happiness, and that's what I hope you find.

I know you said in your email that you don't remember much of anything from that time, but there are a couple of things that I would like to talk to you about. Would you mind answering a few questions some time?

I hope that everything is good with you and that we can be friends going forward. It was good hearing from you…

Shawn

This sounded like a different Shawn than I had held in my mind for so long. Three apologies in one short email. He seemed sensitive and happy I was in love.

I checked my team. They were all handling calls with no problem and not a Sup call in sight. I went back to my workstation and answered his email.

I will help answer questions you have. My memory of faces is lousy, but I think I remember just about everything else.

Yes, I am in love. I married Rick Johnson a few years out of high school. We were together up until a few years ago. Drugs became a major factor in his life and I finally had enough. I am now with someone who thinks I am beautiful. We have been together for a couple of years and I am very happy.

It's good to hear from you.

Dawn

It was such an odd feeling. Shawn had occupied a powerful place in my life for as long as I could remember, first as a friend, then as my first love, and finally as my betrayer. For the last thirty years, he hadn't added anything new to the conversation. Any new elements had been layered onto my memory of him by other people. Now he was here again, a real living person with his own thoughts and perspectives. That complicated things. It was difficult to keep hating him when he was being so reasonable, which kind of made me hate him all over again.

We traded emails the rest of the day. He brought up some of the things that we had done as kids and told me he was hoping to turn our story into a book someday. My take was that he was just trying to get me to think about the happy memories we had shared, so that I would forget the obvious—that he had gotten me pregnant and abandoned me. Evidently he thought I had learned nothing about people and deception since my teen years.

Even so, talking back and forth with him, even via email, felt a little more natural every day. I couldn't help but compare it to when we first became friends after I moved to Washington. It was almost like we both agreed to just put aside all the difficult issues of our separation while we got reacquainted.

Within a few weeks, we were emailing each other seven or eight times a day. We started out just talking about things we had in common—old friends, Mossyrock, 70s music—but eventually we started to share details about our current lives. He told me he had been a real estate broker in Enumclaw for many years, but that the recent economic slump had just about wiped him out. He had three daughters he was proud of. Through it all, I kept my walls up, guarding against emotional involvement.

One night I went back through all the emails we had been sending and saw that I hadn't said one single nice or complimentary thing to him the whole time. He kept coming back for more. Was he paying his penance or was he hoping there might be something else ahead for us? Was it possible he felt that same irresistible pull toward me that I still felt for him, no matter how I tried to deny it?

Finally, he asked me if I held a grudge against him because of the way we had ended. I wrote an answer that said "Grudge? No, a grudge is something small compared to what I've felt about you for the last 30 years. What is the word for something that is ten times as big as a grudge?" I thought better of it, though and deleted it. Instead, I sent this:

I did have anger toward you. I was very young when we were together and I saw you as a manipulative older guy who talked me into things. I thought for the longest time you had ruined my life. I suppose it was easy to think that because you were gone and Mom was always telling me that.

It wasn't until my daughter Dani became pregnant at 15 that I realized that it didn't really happen the way I remembered it. Dani's boyfriend is 19, but she is the boss of that relationship. Over the years I have figured out that most 18-19 year old boys are not very bright. That is why I don't blame you for anything anymore. It's easy for me to blame you for everything, but it's a waste of time.

A lot of what I have thought about this has changed recently. I had told both Connie and Dani the stories about what had happened with us. I didn't tell them about any of the good things that happened, just the bad stuff. I was hoping to scare them from having sex with anyone. Since Dani's pregnant now, I have to admit it didn't work.

Anyway, the way I had told the story, you didn't come out looking very good. I told Dani that I hated you for what you had done to me. She asked me why. I told her because I was an innocent young girl and you took my virginity away. You were the older, smarter one and you manipulated me. She looked at me like I was insane. She couldn't believe I would hold on to that feeling for so long.

Last night I finally told her that I've been talking to you via email. I admitted that I hadn't told her the whole story about us when she was younger and I finally told her the good things that we had shared back then. The first thing she asked was if I saw how stupid it had been to hate you all this time.

The things I have to learn from my children...

He answered me that he didn't mind that I had used him as an example of the boogeyman, but he seemed surprised that I saw things that way. The last time we actually saw each other, we were young, in love, and ready to be together forever. Everything else happened after he was out of the picture. Maybe the impact of that was lost on him.

Meanwhile, at home, things were getting worse and worse with Aaron. Actually, things had been pretty bad for a long time. We had broken up a few times, but since we shared the lease on the house and all the bills, I felt financially dependent on him. After a while, I knew that wasn't enough reason for Dani and me to be miserable all the time, so I picked a fight with him and used that as an excuse to break up. As soon as I did that, I felt free on one hand, but trapped on the other. The house didn't have any extra bedrooms, but I couldn't afford to move out, so I started sleeping on the couch every night.

After sleeping on the couch for a few days, I mentioned it in an email to Shawn. I almost didn't, because I didn't want him to get the mistaken idea that I was interested in being with him, but eventually it came out because he had slowly become what he had been when we were kids—my confidant. Even though we had been emailing each other nonstop for almost a month, we still hadn't talked on the phone yet. I think we were both more comfortable with the extra layer of protection that email provided.

Within a few minutes of getting the email telling him I was sleeping on the couch, he sent me an email that said: *I think it's time for us to talk. Can I call you tonight?"*

I sent him my phone number.

I was working a late shift at ACS that night and had been busy monitoring some of my agents' calls when I remembered Shawn told me that he would call. I checked my phone and, sure enough, there was a voicemail message waiting for me.

"Dawn, it's Shawn."

His voice sounded so much older. Deeper. The boy I knew was gone, but the way he spoke rang bells of familiarity in a deep part of my memory.

"It feels so weird to be calling you like this after all these years." There was a short gap of silence. "Anyway, I'm just at my house, doing nothing. Give me a call if you want to."

I saw that I had only missed his call by a couple of minutes. I hit redial, heard two rings, then that same strange-yet-familiar voice said "Dawn?"

"Hi."

"Are you still at work?"

"Well, I'm at work. Am I actually working? No, not really."

"It's early still, so I'm going to be up for quite a while. Do you want to call me back when you get off?"

"No, this is fine. I've just been working some extra hours tonight. I can be done any time I want. So, go ahead."

"Well, I guess this is a good time for us to get caught up then. Shouldn't take more than a few minutes to cover both our lives for the last thirty years, right?"

"Still a smart-ass, I see."

"Some things never change."

And that was all it took to break the ice, at least a little bit. I still didn't trust him, but it was easy to slip back into our old friendship, insulting and making fun of each other.

He said "I'll go first," and told me about his life. He mostly talked about his daughters Desi, Samy, and Brina. He told me he had been married to their mom for fourteen years, and that it had never been a good match, but that they had stayed together that long for the sake of the girls. When they divorced, she moved with the girls to Arkansas, and he said that he had now made the round-trip drive from Washington to Arkansas more than a dozen times.

"2400 miles, three days, overnight stops in Billings, Montana and Sioux City, Iowa, no sweat," he said. He added that when his wife moved away, he didn't miss her, but being away from his three girls almost killed him.

He said he had dropped out of the University of Washington right after we broke up, went to broadcast school in Seattle, and worked mostly in radio for the next ten years. He had worked at radio stations in Montana, Wyoming, California and Washington. He had quit radio in 1990 because it didn't really pay enough to support a family. In 1993, he started selling real estate in Enumclaw, and he'd been there doing that ever since.

Then he said, "OK, now it's your turn."

"I don't think I want to go now, thank you. My life hasn't been very exciting. I never left Lewis County. I've worked a bunch of dead-end jobs just to get by. There's not much to tell."

"Sure there is. Tell me about your girls."

And so I did. I told him all about Connie and Dani from the time they were little girls until they were all grown up. There was a lot to tell. When I looked at my watch, I saw that we had been talking for almost two hours.

I finished by telling him the story of Dani's pregnancy and how strong she had been about what was going to happen. Talking to Shawn about it, the strong parallels to our story became obvious.

He started to say something, then hesitated and stopped. "What is it?" I asked.

"When we were separated in 1979, we never really got to talk about what happened with our baby. Would it be OK if we talked about it now? There are some things that I would really like to know."

"I guess. What is there to talk about, really?"

I had been lulled into letting my defenses down, but the wall was back up instantly.

"There are just so many blank spots for me. I'd love to fill them in."

"Blank spots? Like what?"

"Well, I got that horrible phone call from Walt and Colleen, telling me you were pregnant. Then I came to see you in Morton but you wouldn't talk to me. The next day we all met in your mom and dad's living room and I agreed not to see you for three years. Then we didn't talk for thirty years, no matter how I tried. I never even knew if you were really pregnant or not."

"I was."

I heard that weird, ghostly silence like you hear only on a cell phone call. It went on for quite a few seconds. I heard him take a deep breath and let it out. When he spoke again, it sounded like he was crying. I didn't understand. How had he not known?

"Dawn, I am so sorry. I'm sorry for you, I'm sorry for me, but mostly I'm sorry for our baby. Your parents had said you were pregnant, but I never knew for sure and no one would talk to me about it. I am so sorry I wasn't strong enough or smart enough to stop that from happening."

"I don't understand. What do you mean 'stop that from happening?'"

"I mean, I did everything I could so that we could keep the baby, but no matter what I said, they wouldn't listen. I told them I wanted to marry you and that we would raise the baby, but they said I ruined your life and you didn't want to see me ever again. I understood that, but when I said that Terri had offered to pay for all the medical expenses if we could put the baby up for adoption, they still wouldn't agree. Over and over, they told me I had two options: pay for the abortion or go to jail. I did everything I could to stop it, but I didn't do enough, and I'm sorry."

His words crushed me. My heart broke, but I had become good at keeping it together.

"Are you saying you wanted to keep our baby?"

"Yes, of course. That's what I came to your volleyball game in Morton to tell you. Didn't you know that?"

"Mom said that the abortion was your idea. That you volunteered to pay for it and that you were glad to be rid of both the baby and me. She said you already had girlfriends in Seattle and that you didn't want to be stuck with a Mossyrock girl and a baby."

There was more silence. "Have you believed that all these years?" he asked, so quietly.

"Yes." My voice grew just as small.

"Oh, Dawn. Oh my God. Then you think... you think that I slept with you, got you pregnant, and then paid for the abortion and disappeared forever."

"Yes."

"Dawn, all I can say is... your mom lied to you. When I lost you and we lost our baby, I lost everything good in my life. My life has felt wrong ever since that day. From that moment until now, there has been a hole in my life that nothing could fill."

Silence stretched out. I was stunned and had no words. I couldn't make my brain function.

I heard Shawn say, "Shit. Shit. Shit!"

I finally found my voice. "Shawn!"

"...Shi—"My voice cut through his and he grew quiet.

I chose my words with all the calm I could gather. "We need to sit down, face to face, and talk."

Falling Slowly

When I hung up the phone I could barely think straight. Everything I ever believed had been pulled out from under me. I suppose all parents lie to their kids at some point, for their own good. But why would Mom lie to me about something this huge, something that changed my life for the worse in almost every possible way?

Shawn sounded sincere to the point that it was easy for me to believe that at least he believed what he was saying, but I still wasn't ready to just accept that my life for the last thirty years had been based on a lie.

Because our schedules wouldn't match up for a few days, we weren't able to get together until that Friday. Shawn said he wanted to take me out to dinner. I wasn't actually scheduled to work that day, but I told him to pick me up at ACS in Tumwater. I felt better knowing I would have friends and support around when I saw him for the first time.

Nervous as I was, I went into work two hours before he was supposed to pick me up. It was a hot day and I wanted to look as good as I possibly could, so I waited until I was there to get dressed, put my makeup on, and straighten my hair. It was a hot, humid day, so I knew if I straightened my hair in the morning it would be frizzy when Shawn arrived.

I was completely ready to go at least a half hour before he was supposed to pick me up. I paced around ACS and listened to everyone make fun of me for being dressed nice with makeup and straight hair. I was starting to get a complex. Did I normally look ugly and frumpy or something?

Finally, I got a text from Shawn saying he was in the parking lot. I took a deep breath, put my sunglasses on, and went outside to see him for the first time in years. When I came out the door, he wasn't where I expected him to be parked, so I had to hunt for him a little bit. I looked to my left and there he was, leaning up against the front of his car, arms crossed, sunglasses hiding his eyes, and wearing that little crooked smirk I had never forgotten.

I walked toward him. No reaction. I realized with a shock that he didn't recognize me! My hair was a lot longer than when he saw me at Bill & Bea's, and it was styled differently.

As I got closer I saw him jump a little bit, like he finally recognized me. He pulled his sunglasses down and peered over them, looking at me appraisingly. He didn't say anything, but his smile widened a little. He gave me a little hug, but it was like two strangers hugging.

"Let's go into Seattle for dinner, OK?" he asked.

Since we were in Tumwater, I thought that was a long ways to go to get dinner, but I said, "Fine. Whatever."

Two minutes later we were on I-5 and heading north. My phone buzzed and I saw it was a text from Sheilah, my best friend in the world that I didn't give birth to.

"You OK? Is he there yet?"

"Yes. Yes."

I hit 'send,' then thought to add *"He's taking me to Seattle for dinner. If you never hear from me again go looking for him."* I was joking. Mostly.

When I looked at Shawn, I realized he was in mid-sentence and I had completely tuned him out.

"...two CD's. I thought it would be cool if we could listen to our music on the drive."

I nodded as if I had been listening or paying attention. He reached down and turned the volume up on the CD that he had put in. *I Will Still Love You* by Stonebolt was playing. I had really grown to hate that song.

"This is the song you asked me to remember that last time I saw you in 1979. Remember?"

"I remember. I don't like it."

"Oh." He deflated a little bit and hit the "next" button on the CD player. *My Angel Baby* by Toby Beau started to play. That was a little better.

"So, now that we're together in one place and talking to each other again, I suppose there are a few things I need to tell you."

Radar up. Hackles raised.

"Really? Like what?"

"Well, it's pretty much the last thing on Earth I want to talk with you about, but I need to talk about my marriage. Adinah and I got married eight years ago. I knew it was a mistake almost immediately and I've been trying to end it for more than five years now."

I knew it. Ooohhh, why do I let myself get sucked in by guys that sound so sincere and are really playing me for a fool? I put on my frostiest smile and said, "Have you ever tried saying 'I want a divorce?'"

"Actually, no. At least not until recently. I finally did last Saturday. It's hard for me to explain why it took me so long to do it. Even though I knew we shouldn't have gotten married, I felt guilty about it and could just never work up the oomph to tell her that."

"I don't know what you've got in mind, Shawn, but I'm not going to be any part of you ending your marriage."

"Everything to do with ending my marriage started years before you and I started talking again. I told her I didn't love her years ago. We'd gone to marriage counseling for two years until I think the counselor gave up on us as hopeless, which we were."

He glanced at me. I gave him nothing. He sighed.

"Dawn, it's been a long time. We don't really know each other anymore..."

"That's right. We don't. And if you think I am that same scared little fifteen-year-old girl you left behind in Mossyrock thirty years ago, you couldn't be more wrong."

"I get that, and thank God. I've grown up. I'm different too. I would have no interest in talking to a young girl. I want to find out who you are now. I know we've been emailing back and forth like crazy, but that doesn't mean we know each other. You don't owe me anything. If you want to have dinner and then say goodbye forever, that's OK."

I still gave him nothing. We rode in silence except for the soundtrack of our teenage lives playing in the background. Once we got to Seattle I was totally lost, but Shawn drove like he knew exactly where he was.

"This is Capitol Hill. It's where I used to live with my sister Terri. We lived just a few blocks away, and every Sunday we would walk down here and go to brunch at Charlie's on Broadway. I thought that would be a good place for us to eat tonight. It's not the fanciest place, but it's got good food."

When we walked inside Charlie's, I liked it immediately. It had the feel of a place that had been there for a while. The maître d' took us to a booth in the corner.

As soon as we sat down, a waiter appeared with water and menus. They were efficient in this place. We both took our sunglasses off and got our first good look at what thirty years had done to us. I studied him as he talked, but honestly, I can't say he was all that familiar. I had read the story he wrote about our meeting at Bill and Bea's, so I knew he had recognized me just by my laugh, but I couldn't say the same.

We both ordered fish and chips. Shawn ordered an iced tea, saying, "I never did learn how to drink," and I ordered a Tequila Sunrise. I had learned how, and felt like I could use the boost. When my drink came, I took a long pull and almost choked. It was so strong I had trouble catching my breath for a second. Maybe I hadn't learned all that much after all.

Shawn was looking at me so seriously. He said, "I have something else that's been bugging me a little bit."

Oh, my God. What else now?

"OK. What?"

"In one of your emails the other day, you said that you had resented me all these years because I was an older guy and I manipulated you into having sex."

"Right. I had wanted to stay a virgin until I got married."

"Right, I know. We both did. But…I have a different memory of how that all played out than you do."

"What do you mean?"

"That one time we were together, on New Year's Eve, it happened because of you, not because of me."

I had absolutely no idea what he was talking about. I just shook my head, but he went on.

"That day, you called me at my Mom and Dad's house and asked me if I was a virgin, remember? Then you told me 'Not for long" or something like that. Then you told me the address of the house to meet you at that night and hung up."

I had to sit there in silence for a second and absorb that. All of a sudden I couldn't really remember the circumstances leading up to us sleeping together. Mom had told me for so long that Shawn had manipulated me that I had long since stopped thinking about how it had actually happened. Then, something clicked in my brain. An image of the fifteen-year-old me popped into my brain, standing in my Mom and Dad's living room, making that exact phone call.

Crap.

"Oh my God. Why hadn't I remembered that until just now?"

Shawn shrugged. "I don't know. You were young. We never got to talk to each other again after that night. I'm sure your mom painted the picture she wanted you to believe and then reinforced it every chance she got. I'm just glad you remember it, or I might think I've gone crazy."

It seemed like every few minutes there was some new revelation. I just wanted to take a minute and catch my breath. The ice in my drink had melted enough that I could take a sip without choking. Our food had arrived long ago, but neither one of us had done more than pick at it. I was moving my coleslaw around with my fork when I looked at Shawn. He was holding his fork in such an odd way—more like a child than a man—that it stirred an old, long-forgotten memory. That simple act, holding his fork in a fist, opened the floodgates in my mind.

Everything came back at once. Laughing, talking, holding each other close. The way he always touched my cheek before he kissed me. Warmth. Safety.

I lost my grip on my fork and it clattered onto my plate. Shawn must have been lost in thoughts of his own, because that startled him. He reached for me across the table, touching my hand. "Dawn? Are you all right?"

So many things that had been just out of my reach came into focus.

"You're my Shawn."

Shawn was smiling. "Yes. I always have been. You see me now."

I nodded and realized I had tears running down my face. Shawn reached out again and put his whole hand around mine, engulfing it.

"I had lost you. I had forgotten. I'm so sorry."

He shook his head, still smiling. "It doesn't matter now."

I knew that was right. It didn't matter. I felt something settle over me that I hadn't felt in so long I forgot what it felt like. I felt at peace. Sitting there in Charlie's on Broadway in Seattle, with Shawn holding my hand like we were teenagers again, was exactly where I was supposed to be. I was with exactly who I was supposed to be with, after all these years. It's hard to explain exactly why or how, but at that exact moment I knew I wasn't going to let Shawn go. I had quit believing in fairy tales and "'happily ever after' when I was fifteen, but at that moment I felt a certainty I hadn't felt since that age.

We realized we had been sitting there for three hours, and it was time to leave. We walked back to the car, and I thought Shawn might reach down and hold my hand again, but he didn't. He did open my car door for me, though, and that was nice.

The ride from Tumwater to Seattle had been awkward and filled with long silences. The ride back felt like we were sitting cross-legged in the side yard again, gossiping about our friends and memories.

By the time we pulled back into the ACS parking lot, it was almost midnight. Dani was waiting for me at home. I had to get up and go to work again early in the morning, but I wasn't quite ready to let go of this feeling we had stumbled upon.

Shawn pulled alongside my Grand Am in the now-deserted parking lot. He put it in park but left the engine running. He looked nervous. I felt completely calm.

He started babbling a little bit, just as he used to do when we were young.

"Thank you for tonight. Getting to see you and talk to you again is like a dream to me. I've thought about you and wondered about you since the day I left your mom and dad's house thirty years ago. Just talking to you and knowing you again brings me peace. Still, I know you've got a lot going on. Dani's going to be having her baby soon. You're going to have to find a new place to live. You've got your job. I don't know if there's room in all that for me, too."

I stared at him and raised my eyebrows. "Are you trying to get rid of me?"

"No! No. I just… I don't want to presume anything. Just because you remember who I am now doesn't necessarily mean…"

"Yeah, my life has worked out so well without you, hasn't it? Turn off the car."

He did. I shifted in my seat and moved closer to him. When he turned back around, our faces were inches apart.

"Dawn. I know there are a lot of things we need to figure out. We have two completely separate lives right now. But, I feel so much for you. I always have. It has never gone away."

"I know. Me too. I feel it. Everything is moving so fast though. A month ago we hadn't talked to each other in thirty years. Until a few hours ago, I didn't know that you were still married. We need to take it slow. Everything will work out just like it's supposed to. But, for now, everything will have to wait. It's late."

He smiled gently and said, "I know." He got out of the car and came around and opened my door. When I got out, he reached out and took my hand and walked me the few feet to my car. When I started to open my car door he reached out and pulled me toward him. He kissed me, filling me with the most intense feeling of déjà vu I had ever experienced. For those few seconds, I was back in the yard after our *Star Wars* date and it was our first kiss all over again. I felt the same explosion of heat and emotion I had then.

"Dawn, I love you."

He literally clapped his hand over his mouth like he hoped he could catch the words before they escaped. It was too late. He looked at the ground, embarrassed. I touched his chin and lifted his eyes to meet mine.

"Taking it slow, remember?"

He nodded, looked a little guilty, and opened my door for me. I smiled, waved, and headed for home.

Years before, I had learned that tears didn't solve anything and so I had given up on them. I had frozen the part of me that might have been tempted to ever cry. Now, driving home with the feel of Shawn's lips still warm on mine, I let them come. There were tears of sadness at everything we had lost, tears of frustration at how easily we had been fooled, and tears of happiness knowing that he had never stopped loving and believing in me.

Beautiful Boy

When I got in to work the next morning, I resolved to keep what had happened with Shawn and me to myself. It all seemed so weird—dating your first boyfriend who you've kind of hated for thirty years, and being pretty thrilled about it—that I didn't want to say anything and have someone rain on my happiness. I must not have done a very good job of hiding it though, because people immediately started to ask me why I was smiling the way I was. Then they started making fun of me, saying they had never actually seen me smile before. I was not amused.

It was like Shawn had forgotten he was a forty-nine-year-old man and had reverted to being a teenager. He wanted to drive from Enumclaw to Tumwater or Chehalis every day. He said that he was glad to make the hour and a half drive just to say hello, but I wouldn't let him. I had to work the rest of the weekend, but I told him that he could come down and we could have dinner on Monday.

At 5:00 on Monday night he was waiting for me, leaning up against the front of the car, smiling. At least he was consistent.

We drove a mile or so to a little Mexican restaurant in Tumwater called El Serape. We both ordered Chile Verde and Shawn ordered another iced tea while I had a grande margarita. We had so much to talk about that it felt like we would never be able to cram it all into one lifetime. Our first few dates involved a lot of comparing notes about what we had been told about each other, and where the discrepancies and lies had been. Shawn was disarmingly honest about everything, admitting to faults and mistakes and taking responsibility for the mistakes he had made, sometimes much more than he needed to.

Those conversations were also intense. We were always

circling the subject of our baby. Each time the subject came up, I saw the hurt in his eyes and knew that the pain I had felt all these years was now a shared burden. His version—that he had wanted both me and our baby—became more credible every time I saw his expression.

When we walked into the warm summer air, I felt lighter than I had in forever. Shawn opened the door for me and leaned down and kissed my neck, giving me goose bumps I also hadn't had in forever.

"Dawn Adele, you fill up my senses."

"Seriously, Patrick Shawn? John Denver? What's next, Barry Manilow?"

He smiled and kissed me. I felt so happy.

We drove back to the ACS parking lot where my car was parked. I felt an overwhelming sense of security and love. Shawn was in the middle of telling me a story about a real estate deal that he had been working on that day, but something else suddenly seemed a lot more important. I reached out and touched his arm.

"Shawn, I love you."

His mouth fell open a little bit. He said, "I will never leave you, unless you send me away."

"Why would I ever want to do that? The best part of my life has been when I'm with you. I love you and I want you with me, always."

"I love you, too, Dawn. I just want you to know what I have always known: I will never leave you unless you send me away. We've both had so many losses in our lives, I want there to be one thing that you know you can count on, and that's me."

He laid his head softly against my shoulder and I saw that he was crying. "You're such a girl," I said.

"You're such a romantic. And hey, whatever happened to 'taking it slow?' Does waiting three whole days before you tell me count as 'taking it slow?'"

"I could take it back, you know."

"No, no, that's all right. I'm perfectly fine with you being unable to contain your love for me."

I hadn't planned on telling Shawn I loved him right then, or for quite a while. Somehow, when I'm with him, my feelings just come out.

Going home that night and sleeping on the couch at the

house I was still sharing with Aaron was uncomfortable, and I'm not just talking about the couch. Shawn drove down the next day, and we looked at rentals around Centralia and Chehalis.

I knew that in his heart, he wanted me to move up to Enumclaw and into his house. It was plenty big enough, but I knew that wouldn't be right. It was way too much, way too soon. Also, when I thought about it, I realized I had never had a place that was just my own. I had lived with Mom and Dad on Damron Road until I moved in with Rick. I wanted to have a place that was mine.

It took us a few days, but we found it; a little duplex in one of the not-so-great neighborhoods in Chehalis. The kindest thing to say about it was that it was very basic. But it had three bedrooms, which meant there was enough room for me, Dani and our new baby that would be showing up in just a few weeks.

Shawn rented a truck and drove it down from Enumclaw with some furniture from his own house. I needed it, since I was leaving almost everything behind. I thought it was better if we made the move while Aaron wasn't home, so I found out when he was going to be gone. Shawn, Dani, Connie and her boyfriend Jamie and I loaded up everything in just a couple of hours.

I was home, at least for the moment.

Dani's due date was in mid-August. When nothing happened by then, her doctor set a date of August 18th to induce labor. We were scheduled to arrive at the hospital at 7:00 AM, so I had my alarm set for 6:00. When it was still dark out, Dani came stumbling into my room, saying she wasn't feeling well. I mumbled a couple of incoherent questions and sent her back to bed until it was time to get up.

In my defense, I am not a morning person. Shawn likes to say that I am not a morning person in the same way that the Titanic didn't have a successful maiden voyage. Shawn says a lot of things that get him in trouble.

When my alarm went off, I remembered what day it was and got out of bed and went to check on Dani. She was up and dressed and walking across the floor when she halfway doubled over. It was a contraction. She had been in labor for several hours by that time; I just hadn't recognized it through the fog of sleep.

We hurried to the hospital and told them that they could forget about inducing her because nature was taking its course.

They put us in a delivery room, and the hard work began. I've always been proud of my girls, but I have never been more proud of Dani than I was that day. It was a hard labor that went on and on through the morning and afternoon. After eight to ten hours of labor, the doctor examined her and decided that the baby's head was turned wrong and it wouldn't be safe to deliver him naturally.

It was a flurry of activity from there, and even though Dani looked scared sometimes, she was as brave as a girl could be. At first they told me they were just going to do a local anesthetic, so I could stay in the room during the Caesarian. They gave me some fresh scrubs and told me to wash up so I could be there.

Soon after that, though, there was something in her vital signs and they decided to do a general anesthetic instead of a local. That meant I got shooed out to the waiting room with Connie, still dressed in the scrubs. I stood outside the operating room for an hour looking like a nurse, I guess, because people were constantly asking me questions.

Then a nurse came out and told us that everything had gone fine. We would be able to go in and see Dani and her healthy baby boy in just a minute. That minute seemed to take a very long time, but we already know that patience isn't my strong suit.

When we went in, the nurse handed me a little bundle with the most beautiful boy in the world wrapped inside. He had dark hair and the most peaceful, handsome little face I had ever seen. I fell in love again, instantly. He was so perfect.

Dani named him Yael. He changed all our lives, but Dani's the most. Growing up in the chaos of my marriage to Rick had been hard on her, and she had been heading down the wrong road since she was eleven years old. Yael changed all that. He inspired her and focused her on the things that were important. She was never the same.

Shawn had to work that day, but drove down as soon as he could. We stood together in Dani's room, holding Yael and marveling at how much we already felt for someone so small. It was one of the best and happiest days of my life.

Once, while I was holding him, I saw Shawn looking at Dani, and then back at me and Yael. He had a sad little smile on his face and I knew what he was thinking. We had missed out on our version of this moment, and we both knew it. It was so sad. Still, here was proof that our children could make better decisions than we ever did.

Grow Old With Me

By the first weekend in September, Shawn and I had been back together for two months. We were still a brand new couple, but at the same time, I felt a growing sense of permanence when we were together. That night sitting in Charlie's, I had felt like I was never going to let him go again if I could help it. That feeling had only grown stronger.

We decided to take the Saturday and drive back down to Mossyrock. Since all four of our parents were dead and neither of us had any relatives left in Mossyrock, there hadn't been much reason for either of us to go back very often. We didn't have anything in particular to do or see, and Mossyrock doesn't have a lot of thrills and excitement. We just wanted to see the old hometown through the perspective of being back together.

We made the two-hour drive arguing about music, movies and all the other stuff we had argued about since 1976. Nothing but the names had changed over the years. We drove through town and I turned to Shawn.

"Alright, that killed about sixty seconds. What do you want to do now?"

"I guess I can see why we used to drive out town or to Longview on all our dates," he said.

We drove past all our old hangouts, but nothing was the same. The Mossyrock Lanes bowling alley looked long since closed down. The G Theater, where we had gone to many movies together, was boarded up. I had no idea what kids did for fun in town in 2009.

We crossed Highway 12 and turned right onto Damron Road. Everything looked strange, even though much of it was unchanged. Shawn actually drove past his old trailer before he stopped and realized what he had done.

"I can't believe I just did that. I drove past my own house."

He backed up and pulled into the side yard where he had parked his Vega all those years before. I looked at my old house. It was different. Someone had remodeled it. It looked nicer, but it didn't look like home.

"You know, we are in Mossyrock," I said. "Sitting in someone else's yard might get us shot at."

"If they do, it'll probably only be with rock salt. It's worth the risk." He pointed out at the side yard. "That's where you became my friend, that's where we had our first kiss, that's where... we became 'us.'"

He put the car in reverse and turned back up the way we had come. Before he got back on the highway, he turned right and slowly drove up the hill to Doss Cemetery.

"How long has it been since you've been up here?" he asked.

"I don't know. Maybe thirty years?"

"What? None of your other boyfriends ever brought you up here? What's wrong with them?"

"To the cemetery? No, none of them ever brought me up here. I wouldn't have let them even if they had wanted to. This was our place."

"I know. It hasn't been that long for me. When I saw you at Bill & Bea's in 2006, I was missing you so bad I drove down here. I didn't even go into town. I just drove up here and sat in the cemetery. I listened to our old songs and... well, it wasn't a very happy time. This is much better."

No argument there.

He turned down the little path that ran alongside the cemetery and drove straight to our old parking spot. "You remember coming here a few times?" he asked.

I looked at him like he couldn't possibly be serious. "Yes..."

"And do you remember what we used to do here?"

"Yes, vaguely."

"Well?"

"Oh, you want to crawl in the back and make out like a teenager? Do you have a chiropractor on permanent retainer? I think we would both need one."

He shrugged. "It's worth the risk to me."

I hit him, then rested my head against his shoulder.

"I never even let myself dream that we could get back here, you know?"

Shawn nodded and turned on the windshield wipers. It was just starting to rain. The stereo was playing the CD he had made just for the trip. It was a very cozy feeling.

All of a sudden, Shawn sat up straight, opened his car door and got out into the rain. "Where are you going?" I asked.

He didn't answer, but walked around the car and opened my door. He got down on one knee in the muddy grass.

"Dawn Adele. I have always loved you. I will always love you. Will you marry me?"

I was surprised, of course. I mean, he had put *Grow Old With Me* by Adam Sandler on the CD he had made for the trip, but he was always doing things like that. I probably should have been more surprised than I was, but on so many levels, it felt like we already were married. I couldn't imagine myself with anyone else ever again.

It took about two seconds for all these thoughts to run through my mind, but when I looked at Shawn, he actually looked like he was holding his breath and waiting anxiously. Could he really have any doubt what I would say?

For the second time in my life, I said, "Yes, Shawn. I will marry you."

This time was a lot happier than the first. The first time, I knew that even though we loved each other and wanted to get married, there was no practical way to make it happen. This time, there was really nothing that could stop us, although there were a few hurdles we had to jump over. For one thing, we were both married to other people. Shawn had everything worked out with his ex, so I wasn't worried about that, but I hadn't so much as spoken to Rick in five years.

That led us to the need to decide what kind of a wedding we wanted. I couldn't imagine running off to Vegas and getting married. I knew I had to have Connie and Dani there, and I was sure Shawn felt the same about his daughters. Still, in 2009, Shawn's real estate was slow and I was just making enough to pay my bills every month. I had no idea how we would pay for a big wedding. Those were all worries for another day.

I kissed Shawn.

"Are you still serious about crawling into the back seat?" I asked.

"I was before I kneeled down here. Now I'm pretty sure it's out of the question."

It's hell getting old.

On the ride back home, we decided to try and have a full wedding, but to put it off for a year or so to give us plenty of planning time. I wanted to have a fall wedding, so by the time we got to my place in Chehalis, we had picked October 16th, 2010 as the date. That gave us fourteen months to get two divorces finalized and plan a wedding for a couple of hundred of our closest friends. No problem.

A few weeks later, Shawn called me at work. "Hey, beautiful one, what are you doing on October 16th?"

I was pretty sure this was a trick question, so I asked, "Which year?"

"This year, of course!"

"Oh. I've got nothin'. Why? What are you doing on October 16th?"

"I'm going to be in Seattle celebrating my pre-versary with you."

"Our what?"

"Our pre-versary. It will be exactly one year before we get married."

"Did you just make that word up?"

"Maybe. Do you think I should trademark it?"

"I wouldn't worry about it. So, you're telling me I need to get that weekend off?"

"Yes. We're gonna party like it's 1979."

When October 16th arrived, I was planning on sleeping in, since nothing good ever happens before noon. At 9:00 AM, Shawn sent me a text that said *Happy Pre-versary. Copyright pending.* I could have killed him. I was awake though, so I texted him back. Much pain has been avoided by the fact that facial expressions don't translate through texts.

I had no idea what we were going to do, but Shawn had it all planned out. It was mid-afternoon by the time we fought through the ungodly traffic into downtown Seattle. Shawn pulled up to valet parking at a hotel called Hyatt Place. When we walked into the lobby I felt like it really was 1979 all over again, and we were two teenagers from the sticks who had run away from home and were hiding out in the big city.

Shawn checked us in and we took the elevator up to the twentieth floor. It was just a normal, nice hotel room, but when Shawn opened the curtains I saw that we had a view of the ferries on Puget Sound. I went into the bathroom to get all my necessities unpacked. By the time I came out, he had transformed the room.

There were a dozen roses arranged in a vase on the writing desk, candles lit all over the room, and he had plugged his iPod into the player beside the bed. Of course, it was playing *Always and Forever.*

"Happy pre-versary, baby," he said. "I've got to tell you that all I can today, because after today they're all just anniversaries. This is the only one of these we'll ever have. So, do you remember when we went up and saw Terri and Tommy that day that I invited you to Prom?"

I nodded.

"Well, that day, Tommy and I wanted to take you into Seattle to see Laserium, but the show was too late. When you were talking to your mom on the phone, I heard her say 'That's a good thing to save for another day.' But we never made it back to Seattle together after that, so that day never arrived. Until today. That's where we're going to celebrate our pre-versary."

Hyatt Place, it turned out, was just a few blocks from the Monorail to Seattle Center. It had been built for the World's Fair in 1962, but it was still up and running. We rode the Monorail and walked hand in hand through Seattle Center toward the towering arches that marked the Pacific Science Center.

Shawn bought us two tickets to something called *Laser Floyd* and we were the first ones in line. Shawn always likes to be early. When they opened the doors to the Laserium, I saw that it was just a big planetarium, with a few seats scattered in the back and open carpeting everywhere else.

"The seats are where the old people sit," Shawn said.

"And…"

"No. We are not old people. We'll be lying down here, just like we would have in 1978."

Shawn laid down on carpeting that had seen better days and could have used a good vacuuming. The seats were looking better and better to me, but when he looked up at me with that goofy

I'm-still-kind-of-a-teenager grin on his face, I knew I was done for. I sat down and leaned back against Shawn's chest, using him a pillow.

When the music started, a self-announced 'laser technician' started bouncing laser images off the ceiling of the planetarium in time to the music. Since it was all Pink Floyd music, which is pretty spacey to begin with, it was easy to get lost in it. Song blended into song and I got completely sucked into the experience, floating along with the music.

When the last note faded away, people applauded and Shawn sat up. He looked very satisfied. It had been important to him to fulfill the promise to take me that he had made all those years ago.

"There are a lot of other things that I've dreamed about doing with you, but our budget for this weekend was pretty limited, so we had to settle for Laserium for now."

I smiled at him, shook my head and told him the truth. "It was perfect."

A few months later, Shawn called me and said "So, what do you have planned for Valentine's Day?"

Planning things is much more up his alley than mine, so I said, "As usual, I've got nothin'."

"Check with the boss and see if you can get it off, OK? I've got plans for the both of us."

Valentine's Day fell on a weekend that year, and weekends were always the toughest to get off, but I begged and traded shifts until I was off on February 13th and 14th.

A few weeks before that, Shawn was down at my place in Centralia. I was cleaning up the dishes from supper and Shawn was on the computer in the living room.

"Hey, baby, can you come here for a second?"

I grabbed a dish towel and went to see what he wanted. He had a Craigslist ad up, with a picture of a gorgeous white gold diamond ring.

"I'm just starting to think about a ring for you, but I don't know what you like. What do you think about this one?"

When he had asked me to marry him at Doss Cemetery, it had been completely spontaneous and unrehearsed, so he didn't have a ring to give me. I asked him if he still had the little gold rings he bought in 1978, but he said he thrown those out of his car window on I-5 when I wouldn't talk to him on my eighteenth birthday.

When I looked at the picture of the ring I immediately fell in love with it. It was elegant and so beautiful, with dozens of tiny diamonds around the band and an ideal-cut diamond that was almost a full carat. It was everything I ever wanted or hoped for in a ring. Then I snuck a look at the price and knew that it was way outside the price range of what he could afford.

"It's beautiful. It really is. But that's more ring than I need."

"Oh, I know. I'm not intending to buy that particular ring. I just wanted to see if you liked that style or not."

"Yes. I can definitely say I like that style."

A few days later, he told me that he had actually called the seller on that ring but that it had already been sold. I wasn't heartbroken, since I knew it was out of our price range anyway.

Valentine's Day weekend had very typical Seattle February weather. There was complete cloud cover, and it was cold but not freezing, with occasional spitting rain and blustery. Shawn had gotten us reservations in downtown Seattle again, this time at the Grand Hyatt. He said he was taking me somewhere nice for dinner that Saturday night, so we had gone to the mall and found a new dress for me and a new suit for him.

I waited in the lobby while he got us checked in, and when he came back from the front desk, he had a little smile on his face that I had grown to recognize.

"What are you up to?"

"Nothing at all." I knew it was a lie, though I was probably going to forgive him for it. "Are you ready to go up to our room?"

We stepped into the elevator and heard an easy-listening version of *Stairway to Heaven*. "That kind of kills me," Shawn said, "but in a way it's another full-circle moment."

Up on the 27th floor, he used the electronic key to open the door. When I walked in, I was pretty sure we were in the wrong room. It was a suite with a sitting area and kitchenette, a full master suite with a huge marble bathroom. It was bigger than the little duplex I shared with Dani and Yael in Chehalis.

I looked at Shawn, wondering if he had robbed a bank the day before to finance this, but he just shrugged and smiled.

"Never question a miracle, that's what I always say."

"Oh, is that what you always say? I've never heard you say

that before."

"What do you mean? You just did."

He opened the curtains. We were high up enough to have an incredible view looking out at the Space Needle.

"Hurry, though," he said. "We've got people to do and places to see, or something like that."

"I'll hurry if you'll tell me where we're going."

"If you don't hurry, we won't be going anywhere, because we'll be late."

Sometimes I felt like I was hanging out with the Mad Hatter from *Alice in Wonderland.* I hurried though, because I wanted to see where we were going next. Shawn said not to get dressed up yet, but just to dress warm.

A few minutes later we were back in the car, headed south from downtown. Soon we pulled alongside Boeing Field, well south of the urban core. I really, truly had no idea where we were going. Shawn stopped the car in front of a building that said 'Seattle Helitours.'

"OK, OK, it might not be my best idea. I know you're a little scared of heights. But still, I thought it would be cool. Not to mention, I got a Groupon for it. How could I resist?"

The helicopter ride turned out to be awesome and not scary at all. The pilot was a great guide, showing us all around the city and even hovering at eye level with all the tourists on the observation deck of the Space Needle. Shawn had lived in a bunch of different places around Seattle over the years, so he kept pointing to a group of buildings and saying "I lived there, and there." I kept nodding like I could really tell which ones he was talking about.

When we got our feet back on solid ground, we headed back to our suite and got changed for dinner. Since it was a Saturday night and the night before Valentine's Day, I knew it was going to be crowded wherever we went.

We got dressed in our new clothes and rode the elevator down to the lobby, but instead of going outside, we went through a little entrance into the Ruth's Chris Steak House that was attached to the Grand Hyatt. The place was beyond crowded. Every table was full and the waiting area was overflowing with people clear out onto the street. Shawn went to the maître d' station, and thirty seconds later we were on our way to our table. I don't know how he does those things.

I had never been to Ruth's Chris before, but Shawn just told me I was about to get the best steak of my life. We both ordered the petit filet mignon and I had to admit he was right. After we split a piece of cheesecake for dessert, I sat back in my seat and sighed. It had been a wonderful, but very long day, and I was exhausted.

Shawn stood up from the table and I thought he was heading for the bathroom, but he dropped down on one knee right in the middle of the aisle. All the tired left me. I was on full alert. There had been the constant noise of conversations and people bustling all around us, but when everyone saw Shawn get down on one knee, it got very quiet. I saw people pointing at us and whispering.

"Dawn Adele, for the third and final time, I want to ask you: will you marry me?"

He produced a small white box and opened it to reveal the exact ring he had shown me on the computer weeks earlier.

"Why do you keep asking me this? I already told you 'yes!' And I thought you said those rings were sold!"

"I did, and they were. They were sold to me." He's full of surprises. Always has been. Will be forever.

Shawn slipped the rings on my finger. There were four men sitting right behind us on their own Valentine's Day date, and they all stood and applauded. Soon, people all around us were clapping and cheering.

One of the men who had started the cheering said, "Show us how you did!" so I lifted my hand up and showed off the ring to more applause.

Shawn got up off his knee and kissed me. When he sat down, I held the rings out so that they caught the light of the candle on the table. I couldn't ever have hoped for a more perfect ring.

"I hope that's the last time I have to do that, because these old knees aren't what they used to be."

Happily, that was indeed the last time he had to get down on one knee. This one took.

At Last

The rest of 2010 was so busy that there were times I wouldn't have been surprised to pass myself going the other way on the freeway. Even so, life was better than I could ever remember.

In late May, Shawn and I got away for a few days and drove down to Monterrey, California. Other than our little one-night trips into Seattle, it was our first vacation together. I've heard people say that if you want to know someone, go on a long car trip with them. If that's the case, then we are in for a happy life together. We listened to audio books and music and stopped at every roadside attraction that grabbed our attention. We didn't make the greatest time in the world, but we had so much fun.

We needed the break, because the rest of the summer was incredibly hectic. After six years of not speaking a single word to him, I finally worked up the nerve to approach Rick about getting a divorce. I had hoped that after so many years of non-communication, feelings would have cooled and getting the divorce would be easy. I sent Rick an email telling him I was finally ready to file for the divorce and that I didn't want anything other than the dissolution. I didn't hear anything for the longest time, and when I did, I was shocked.

Rick sent an email back lamenting the divorce and saying he had always believed we would get back together someday. This, despite the fact that we hadn't spoken in six years and that our marriage itself had been a failure in every way a marriage can be, aside from producing our two beautiful daughters.

Eventually I just hired a lawyer and instructed him that as long as we got the divorce finalized as quickly as possible, we would give up any other consideration I might be entitled to.

Shawn's divorce was finalized in April, and everything was falling into place for our wedding.

Everything but money, of course. When we put our guest list together, we found we couldn't cut it down to fewer than 150 people. Our wedding budget was more suited to a guest list of about twelve. Shawn has a knack for finding bargains, though, and every time something new came up, we put our heads together and figured a way to make it happen the way we wanted.

As if handling all our legal affairs and planning a wedding wasn't enough, somewhere along the line Shawn and Jerry Weible got together and started planning a KISS II reunion. Because Mossyrock High School was so small, they didn't always have individual class reunions and instead just had an 'All School Reunion' every five years, including 2010. One of the planners contacted Shawn and asked him if they wanted to put on the old costumes and makeup and make a special appearance at one of the parties. Because it was Jerry and Shawn, that little 'special appearance' had somehow ballooned into them doing four entire concerts on the Friday and Saturday of the reunion. Oh, and they wanted to do it at the G Theater, which had been closed for many years and would require renovations before it could be used again.

When Shawn first started talking about it with Jerry, I was all for it. I thought I could get some pictures that I could use as blackmail material for years to come. I had seriously underestimated Shawn's ability to be embarrassed by things that would kill a normal person. I knew I had miscalculated when Shawn started posting their practice pictures on his own Facebook page.

The reunion and first KISS II concert in thirty-two years were scheduled for July 30th in Mossyrock. I probably shouldn't have been surprised when I got my court date for my final divorce hearing with Rick, also on July 30th. Oh, and after seven years of working there, I had given my notice at ACS and my last day was... July 30th. I was pretty sure that if I survived that day, then no stress would ever kill me.

In the end, it wasn't all that bad. My divorce hearing went off without a hitch. Walking out of that courtroom, I felt a burden lift off my shoulders that had been there so long that I had come to accept it as part of myself. My last day at work at ACS was emotional but not bad.

When things were at the very worst in my life, the people I worked with at ACS had become my family. They looked out for me, supported me, and told me things were going to get better. Now things had. I loved so many of them, but I was going to move to Enumclaw after the wedding and it didn't make any sense to drive all that way every day. Still, I was going to miss them.

And the KISS II concert? What is there to say about four people—some of them in middle age—wearing spandex costumes, platform shoes, full-face makeup and lip-syncing to thirty-year-old songs? I didn't know if anyone would actually show up, but they did, and it was a blast. Just like the old days, some of the old people walked out, complaining the whole thing was "too damn loud!" Shawn and Jerry wouldn't have had it any other way.

With all of our legal issues behind us and the concerts out of the way, I was finally able to focus on getting ready for the wedding. Because our guests would be coming from Mossyrock, Centralia/Chehalis, Enumclaw, and all around the region, we had chosen the most central venue we could manage: Heritage Hall on the Thurston County Fairgrounds in Olympia. It was a cool old building that looked like a log cabin. Since our theme was going to be 'Fall,' that would fit right in.

We checked out some caterers to see what it would cost to cater a decent dinner for 150 people. We learned that this would have consumed the entire wedding budget. Shawn said not to worry. He had been a short-order cook when he was a kid, and he was sure that he and a few volunteers could feed everyone for just a few hundred dollars. He's a madman, but a very resourceful madman.

Shawn and I bought most all of the decorations by driving around to dollar stores and using our imagination, but we were still missing a lot of things. Then our friend Sherry Blakely from high school offered to help. She got in touch with us and said that she planned a lot of weddings, and that as her wedding gift to us, she would provide a lot of the decorations needed to make everything look perfect.

I chose Connie to be my Maid of Honor. Dani, my best friend Sheilah, and Shawn's youngest daughter Sabrina would be my Bridesmaids. Shawn picked his daughter Samy to be his "Best Man". Yes, he was aware that his daughter was not really a man, but Shawn has never been one to be ruled by tradition. He chose Jerry Weible, Dani's boyfriend Daniel, and Connie's boyfriend Jamie to be his Groomsmen. Yael and Samy's daughter Millie would be our ring bearer and flower girl.

Every time some new expense popped up, like the wedding cake or the flowers for the ceremony, I would call Shawn and he would say, "Don't worry. We'll figure it out." I don't know if "we" figured it out, or if our friends just all felt sorry for us, but every time, we somehow managed to find a solution.

On the night of the rehearsal dinner, everything we had been planning for a year seemed to come together. I admit, 'rehearsal dinner' might be kind of an overstatement. We asked as many people as we could think of to show up and help us schlep tables and chairs and decorations around, and we ordered pizza, pop and beer. Jessica Coen, one of my best friends from ACS, took charge of getting everything organized. She even volunteered her husband Josh to be our wedding DJ. It took us a few tries to get the tables laid out right, but by the end of the night, everything looked like it was ready for a wedding.

The next day, Shawn got to the hall early and started cooking. Jeff Hunter, another friend from high school and the Stage Manager for KISS II, showed up early and pitched in. Shawn told me that he had so much help in the kitchen that he was able to escape for a few minutes and write his vows for the ceremony. I had to laugh a little at that, since Shawn says I am the one who puts things off, and I had prepared my vows months ago.

Finally all the preparations were done; the tables were full of people we loved, and I could relax at least a little and enjoy the ceremony that I had been planning for a year and awaiting for a lifetime.

I had been hoping that my big brother Brian would make it up from California so that he could walk me down the aisle and give me away, but he couldn't make it. Instead, I asked Jerry if he would do it. All those years ago, I had two 'big brothers' at Mossyrock High School. Now I was marrying one of them, and the other one was giving me away.

Since the middle of October can be stormy in Western Washington, we got very lucky with the weather. There were patches of blue sky. It was actually warm enough outside that some people were complaining it was hot inside the hall. Since we had been worrying about what would happen if we had an early snowfall, that was a good problem to have.

Naturally, Shawn had spent months picking out the music for the ceremony. He said the hard part wasn't so much picking out what songs to play, but which to leave out. He compromised a little by making a special playlist that Josh played while people were being seated and waiting for the ceremony to start.

We had asked Jerry and Lynn Weible's daughters Brittany and Morrigan to be our candle-lighters, and they walked in while *Into My Arms* by Nick Cave and the Bad Seeds was playing. That wasn't one of our songs, but Shawn said that in the years we were separated it had made him think of me almost more than any other song. I had picked *Red Like a Rose* by Alan Jackson for Connie and the bridesmaids to walk in to. Then Samy and the groomsmen entered to Don Mclean's *And I Love You So*. Did I mention that Shawn is a little bit of a romantic?

When the whole wedding party except for Jerry and I were in place, there were a few seconds of silence, then Josh played the Etta James song *At Last*. I stood at the entrance to the hall, looking at so many people who had traveled from far and wide to celebrate with us. I looked to my left and saw all my friends from ACS who had gotten me through so many hard times. Standing at the front, waiting to officiate, was Sheilah's husband Darren. They had given me shelter when the storms in my life were at their very worst and I would love them both forever. There were also four daughters standing there now, where there had only been two before.

And most of all, there was Shawn. When I looked at him, I saw the same skinny, curly-headed boy I had first met thirty-four years before, wearing the same crooked smile as always. I felt all the stress and pressure of the wedding fade away as I focused on him. Even when I blamed him for everything bad in my life, I was never able to forget about him. Now, knowing the truth about everything—and knowing I was going to spend the rest of my life with him—was the best feeling I had ever known.

Jerry and I walked slowly down the aisle. Everywhere I looked I saw smiles and tears, often at the same time. I felt my throat thicken as well, but I had spent way too much time on my makeup to cry now. When we reached the front of the hall, Jerry unhooked my arm and put my hand in Shawn's. It was a good thing he wasn't wearing makeup, because there were tears on his face already.

I faced Shawn and listened as Darren talked about the solemnity of the union we were entering into and the miracle of second chances. He asked us if we had vows we wanted to make to each other. I knew I would be nervous, so I went first. I had written my vows months before, but when the moment arrived, I just took Shawn's hand, looked him directly in the eye, and spoke from my heart.

"What a journey—just a few years ago, I never would have believed I could be standing here with you. If we hadn't been separated by fate, I believe we would still be together today, but I don't know if we would have this same appreciation and love for each other. You are my best friend, my love, my soulmate. Between us, we have brought five of the most beautiful and strong women into the world: our daughters, our family. We have a love for each other that grows stronger every day.

"I have two promises: I promise to thank God every morning for bringing you back to me, and I promise to appreciate everything you are and everything you do for me. Thank you for coming with me on this journey."

We never broke our gaze as we looked past each other's eyes, into souls. I was making a lifetime vow that would never be shaken.

Shawn reached inside his tuxedo jacket and retrieved a piece of paper and his glasses.

"Dawn Adele, I love you more each day. That means I love you more at this moment than I ever have before, yet this is the least I will ever love you in our life together. These are my vows: I vow to always get things down off the top shelf for you without making fun of you because you can't reach it. I vow to always open doors for you, even your car door when it's raining really hard. I vow to bring you your first cup of coffee every day for the rest of your life. Most important to you, I vow to always be your protector from spiders large and small. Most important of all, until I take my last breath, I will never leave you."

Thirty-two years after Shawn first asked me to marry him, Darren said, "You may kiss the bride. Ladies and gentlemen, for the first time anywhere, it is my honor to present Mr. and Mrs. Shawn and Dawn Inmon."

That sounded good to me.

It had been my idea to have the DJ play Stevie Ray Vaughan's *The House is Rockin'* as our exit music. It kind of offset all of Shawn's romantic songs at the beginning of the wedding. And besides, we were old, but we weren't dead, and we were going on our honeymoon.

We stood in the fading sunshine that had blessed our special day and greeted everyone in attendance. Okay, maybe at someone else's wedding we would have greeted them. Instead, Shawn and I laughed, hugged, cried a little, and celebrated with every person that came through our receiving line.

We started the reception off with our first dance as a married couple. I had picked *The Air That I Breathe* by The Hollies for several reasons. For one, it summed up everything I was feeling. After finally getting to marry Shawn, there was nothing else I needed. Also, when we were just kids and I told him this was my new favorite song, he told me that I could only have one favorite song at a time. I had to remind him one last time how wrong he had been back then.

When Shawn took me in his arms and led me around the empty dance floor, I was transported back to when we danced to *Always and Forever* in his mom's living room after our Prom. I had thought that was the happiest I could ever be. I had been wrong.

Just the Two of Us

It was late by the time we were ready to leave Heritage Hall. Part of doing a big wedding on a tiny budget is sticking around after the reception and cleaning up to make sure you get your deposit back. There are two great times to find out who your real friends are: the day you move, and when you have to clean up after a party for 150 people. We found out that a lot of our old friends are real friends, because we had a lot of help. In the end, we also had way too much food, beer and wine, so no one went home empty-handed.

We walked out to find that the kids had decorated our car for the honeymoon with condoms, negligees and by writing "Just Married" on our back window.

Our suitcases were already packed and in the trunk, but Shawn was still in his tuxedo, so we stopped by my place so he could change. He looked good in his tux, but a lot more like my Shawn in his Beatles T-shirt, faded jeans and tennis shoes.

Just as we were ready to get on I-5 and head south, we both realized that we hadn't eaten a single thing all day, not even at our own wedding dinner. We had been too busy talking with friends to eat. Our first meal as husband and wife was served through the drive-through window at Jack-in-the-Box around 10:30 that night.

We spent our first night at a 100-year-old hotel in Portland, Oregon called The Governor. It was old, but really cool and beautiful. Not that it mattered, really. After the day we'd just had, we probably could have stayed at a Motel 6 and not noticed much difference.

The next morning, Shawn fulfilled his wedding vow by waking up before me and running to a coffee shop to get me a hazelnut latte. It didn't take me long to adjust to a life of being spoiled by my new husband. I think I got there in one day.

We spent the first full day of the honeymoon driving Highway 101 down the Oregon Coast. I had no idea where we were going, which was very freeing. Earlier that year we talked about going to Hawaii, but eventually we realized we could have the wedding or the honeymoon, but not both. In fact, at one point, Shawn said that we might not be able to do anything at all.

Then Jerry and Lynn Weible stepped in and told us they wanted to give us our honeymoon as their wedding present. They owned a timeshare that allowed them to book resorts all over the country, so they worked with Shawn to come up with an itinerary for us, but I truly had no idea what it was. I had made the mistake of telling Shawn I wanted to be surprised, so now it would take high-level torture techniques to get any information out of him. It didn't matter where we were going. We were together, we were finally married, and there was a long road ahead of us.

We couldn't have been bigger tourists. We stopped at every lookout and took dozens of pictures of each other with the Pacific Ocean as the backdrop. We stopped at the Trees of Mystery in Klamath, Oregon and took our picture in front of the huge statue of Paul Bunyan and Babe, the Blue Ox. Shawn felt it was necessary to point out that although he often called me "Babe," it wasn't in reference to *that* Babe. I thought it was necessary to chase him around the car a little bit, but I couldn't catch him. He is faster than he looks.

My favorite stop of the day was at the Legend of Bigfoot Store. There was a life-size statue of Bigfoot out by the road, and lots of T-shirts, postcards, and cheap jewelry. I walked out a happy girl with a sweet Bigfoot T-shirt and a peace sign necklace for under twenty bucks.

We even took the cheesiest detour possible—literally. We stopped at the Tillamook Cheese Factory and took a tour. Who knew making cheese could be so fun? I guess to some people this sounds like the worst road trip since the Griswolds went on *Vacation,* but it was the perfect way to start our trip.

We spent the second night in a little hotel called the Anchor Beach Inn in Crescent City, California. It was a pretty basic little place and a pretty basic motel stay, except for one thing: it was our second night as man and wife, and I'll just say we weren't nearly as tired as we had been the night before. It was a good night.

By early afternoon the next day, we checked in to the condo the Weibles had reserved for us in Clear Lake, California. Neither of us had ever heard of the place before, but it took our breath away. The condo was elegant and beautiful and when we walked out on our front patio, we looked right at Clear Lake. Shawn put his arms around me and we tried to take a mental picture that would last forever.

We stayed two perfect days in Clear Lake doing a lot of nothing but resting, relaxing and recovering from the stress of, well, everything. As it turned out, Shawn is a pretty good cook. He barbecued steaks and made us what he called his 'perfect baked potatoes' each night.

The next day we drove all the way down to Oceanside, California. Our plan was to use Oceanside as a base of operations to go down to San Diego, or up to Los Angeles to see the sights. Our plan lasted until we pulled into Oceanside and fell in love all over again. We were staying at another one of the Weibles' condos, so that was perfect, but it was also just the town itself that charmed us.

The first night, we went into town and found a little diner straight out of a 1950s movie. It wasn't like one of those kitschy, nostalgic, built-in-the-nineties-to-look-like-the-fifties sort of diner though. It was one of those places that had been a diner in the fifties, and hadn't changed even in 2010.

Not surprisingly, one of Oceanside's best features was that it lived up to its name. It had a long sandy beach and a half-mile long pier right off the downtown area. Even though it was the middle of October, we spent every afternoon swimming in the Pacific and lying out on towels on the beach.

The second night in Oceanside, we went to a street fair. There was a live band playing '70s and '80s songs. We got our food and sat at a table listening to the band and watching a table full of homeless people. It looked like they had all their possessions in the world with them. They were laughing and joking and were the first ones on the dance floor every song. The thought occurred to me that if you had to be homeless, there were worse places to be than Oceanside, California; although that's probably not the motto the city fathers want to promote.

In the end, we never went north or south during our stay.

When we left to go to our next stop, we were about a mile north of town when Shawn looked at me in all seriousness and said: "I think I'm about ready to go back. How 'bout you?" We didn't, though. We had one more stop ahead of us before we had to go back to our real life. We drove an hour or so north and stayed at another resort in Anaheim, right next to Disneyland. When I was a little girl living in Southern California, I loved going to Disneyland. I hadn't been back in a long time and Shawn had never been there. He told me that when he felt banished from Mossyrock in 1978, he came to see his sister in Los Angeles. He drove by Disneyland, but he didn't have any money to get in.

Shawn thought that he might not actually like Disneyland all that much now that he had a chance to see it, but I had faith that happiest place on earth could win him over.

We got up early and were among the first people inside the gate. It was slightly rainy that day, which seemed to work to our advantage. Lots of people seemed to be waiting out the rain, which meant that there were no lines at all, even for the Pirates of the Caribbean, the Haunted Mansion and Space Mountain.

Our only miscalculation was trying to do Disneyland and California Adventures, the 'new' part of Disneyland, all in the same day. It was mid-afternoon by the time we made it over there, the sun was out and the lines were long. Still, we managed to do the Grizzly River Run twice, getting soaked both times, which felt kind of good. As we were walking out of the park, we walked past the rollercoaster called California Screamin'. Shawn said, "I was thinking about going on that one, but it looks pretty fast and pretty scary. I don't think you'd be able to do it."

He was well aware that there was no better way to get me on a rollercoaster. There wasn't much of a line for it, and five minutes later we were seated and ready for blast-off. And, for some reason, blast-off didn't come and didn't come. Every second that ticked by, the more I convinced I became that something had gone wrong and the less I wanted to go. Finally, after sitting there for four hours, or four minutes—I forget how long it actually was—we took off. Whatever sense I had left was officially scared out of me. It was time to go back to the condo.

We stopped on the way back and got Chinese takeout. We sat on our balcony overlooking Disneyland, feet propped up, and ate General Tso's Chicken. We watched the fireworks over the parks.

It was the ideal ending to our day and our honeymoon. I reached over and held Shawn's hand.

If we had been together since we were teenagers, I know we still would have appreciated good moments like this. I just don't think we would have appreciated the depth of goodness there is in being with your one perfect person unless you have lived your life for so long without him or her.

How Much I Feel

Our 'happily ever after' really started when we got back from our honeymoon and merged our households into our new normal life. I moved out of the Chehalis place and into Shawn's big house on Bondgard Avenue in Enumclaw.

I was in a new town where I knew only Shawn, and I went looking for work. I got lucky and found a part-time job in early 2011 at the local paper, the *Enumclaw Courier-Herald*, assisting the Circulation Manager. When she retired, I took over and became the new Circulation Manager, which is a pretty great job. It was less than a five-minute commute from our house, had good benefits, and the work was actually kind of fun most of the time.

Things remained tough financially for us through the first part of 2011. The real estate market was still not good, and although I liked my new job, it was never really going to make us rich. That meant we struggled financially, but it didn't transfer over into the other parts of our lives and it didn't bother me. I was poor when I was a kid and poor all my life as an adult. It didn't take a lot of adjusting to being poor now. This poverty was different though. Being poor with a partner made everything easier. It didn't matter that we didn't have any money to do anything. I was happier going home to a quiet dinner with Shawn every night than I had ever been doing anything else.

The tough times came to a head in December of 2011 when we lost our house to foreclosure. Shawn bought it at the peak of the market in late 2006 and the payments were more than he could handle when the market crashed around his ears. Our house was foreclosed on the second week in December and we had thirty days to find a new place to live. Shawn was sad to see the house go back to the bank, of course. He never wanted to default on it, but had no way to avoid it.

As with almost everything, there was a silver lining. Shawn had lived in that house with his ex-wife, and I couldn't manage to be as sad as he was to see it go. No matter what we did to that house to make it our own, there was always the knowledge that it hadn't always been ours. That would have never gone away.

Shawn's favorite saying is "Jump, and a net will appear." That was true for us in this case, just like it has so often been. The very first day we went out to look at homes, we found the absolutely perfect house for us to rent. It had three bedrooms, so we had plenty of room when the kids and grandkids came to visit. It had a big deck for summer barbecues, a fenced yard for our two chocolate Labs and a gorgeous view of Mt. Rainier out our back windows. We took it as soon as we walked in, and I knew that we were finally home in a place that was completely ours.

There were two more important things that happened in 2012, and that will at last bring our story full circle.

The first came when Shawn published the story he had written about our life and our love, called *Feels Like the First Time,* on September 4th. He had started writing it two days after we ran into each other in December of 2006, so it had taken him five and a half years to finish. When I would ask him how he was coming on his book, he would often say, "How can I write the ending when we haven't lived it yet?"

I guess he finally thought we had lived enough of our own happy ending that he could call the book finished and publish it. The response to that book went far beyond anything we were hoping for. The overwhelmingly positive response to that book led directly to this one. Time and again, people would ask questions that weren't answered in the first book. Shawn always told them, "I didn't answer that question because this was my story and I never knew the answer either. If you want to know the answer to that, we'll have to wait until Dawn decides to tell her own story in her own book." Well, this is that book, and I hope I have answered at least most of the questions.

The most important thing that happened came right after that, when Dani, Daniel and Yael decided to make their family status a fact of law. Less than two years after we produced our own wedding, we were back in wedding planning mode. On the day of the wedding, Shawn was again in the kitchen, preparing to feed a hundred people on a limited budget.

When it was time for Dani to walk down the aisle, I couldn't hold back my tears. I had loved her since the moment she was born, but she had never been more beautiful. I watched her come down the stairs and walk to Daniel and Yael.

Watching them exchange their vows, I knew this wedding was happening because she had been strong. She questioned authority when it was necessary and stood up for what she believed in. Dani and Daniel had accomplished what Shawn and I had not. We could never go back and fix everything that happened thirty years before, but it was a good, healthy feeling to watch the next generation get it right.

In his book, Shawn said that when we were first together, it was like the world's longest sleepover. More than three years later, I'm happy to say that is still true. We still argue about songs, movies and television shows just like we did as kids sitting in the side yard. I have a hunch that when we are in our eighties and sharing a room in a nursing home, we'll still be having tickle fights and driving the orderlies and our kids crazy.

All my life, people told me that the love I shared with Shawn wasn't real, that love didn't work that way in the real world. For the longest time, I believed them. In so doing, I lost my belief, both in love and in Shawn. I know how insanely lucky we are to have found each other again, that we might prove that wrong forevermore. It's not only possible to have that crazy in-love feeling in your stomach, and feel ultimately content and happy going to sleep next to the person you love every night...

I am, finally, getting the chance to live it.

Afterword –
Love Will Find a Way

I know if there's one question I've left unanswered, it is why Mom acted the way she did toward Shawn. Since Mom passed away almost thirty years ago now and I never talked to her about it before she died, I will never know the answer for certain.

The best I can do is shine a little light on who she was and how she thought. She was raised in a very strict home that she escaped by getting married when she was seventeen. That marriage was a miserable one. When she married a second time, she chose someone she could control almost completely. Her need for control extended to me as well. She raised me to accept her word at face value and never to question authority. I swallowed everything she told me, even when it flew in the face of all evidence around me, and I paid a heavy price for it. That's why I raised my own girls to question everything, no matter who said it.

As to why she disliked Shawn so much, I'm less clear on that. The best I've been able to figure is that she saw that Shawn and I were becoming more and more committed to each other and she felt like she was losing control over me. Once Shawn was gone, she seemed to care much less about where I was, who I was with and what I was doing.

In the end, my best revenge against anyone who has ever harmed me is by living well. Shawn has kept his wedding vows. He still brings me my first cup of coffee every morning. He still opens my car door for me and takes care of spiders both large and small. Sometimes he fails a little bit there because he doesn't kill them but instead catches them in his bare hand—*shudder*—and releases them outside.

I go to sleep every night cuddled up with the best friend I've ever had. He wakes me up with a kiss every morning.

In the end, there is nothing better than that.

Acknowledgements

Many people had a hand in making this book what it is.

It all started with Dawn. Since the basics of this story had already been told in *Feels Like the First Time*, the only way this book would be worthwhile was if she was willing to open her heart and soul and be completely vulnerable to all my endless probing and questions. She did that and more, helping me shape her story into this book. She has always been my soulmate and lifetime love, but after writing her story, I love her and appreciate her more than ever.

J.K. Kelley, who had provided impeccable proofreading on *Feels Like the First Time*, took over the Editor's chair for this book. He was with me from the earliest planning stages right through to his writing of the blurb that is on the back of the book. He helped me more than he could ever know by suggesting that I read *Jane Eyre* just as I was starting to write this book. It was in Jane's earnest voice that I heard echoes of Dawn's own. J.K. has the uncanny knack of taking a tangled sentence and making it flow with just a few changes. I am so lucky to have him serve as my editor.

Linda Boulanger from TreasureLine Publishing once again provided the stunning cover image for the book. She and I worked together on it for months, before it all came together the night before our deadline. She is the most patient, giving, creative person I could ever hope to work with and I hope she never fires me as a client. I don't know what I'd do without her.

Chris Guthrie from Open Book Editors did an outstanding job of proofing the final copy of the manuscript and catching any remaining misplaced punctuation and dialogue. Thank you, Chris, for doing such an excellent job.

Ellen Sallas from The Author's Mentor did an outstanding job on the formatting of both the paperback and e-book versions. Without her, it wouldn't look like a book!

Finally, an important part of any book is my beta readers. They read and give helpful reader feedback on an earlier, rougher draft. This book is better for having been read by: Karen Lichtenwalter, John Draper, Debby Knudtzon, Sherry Eddy, Craig Luddington, Veronica Gann and Laura Heilman, Devy Rains. Thank you for all your invaluable feedback.

My biggest thank you is to you, the reader. I have been so touched and humbled by learning so many of your stories and learned of the parallels between our story and yours. Thank you for being part of our lives.

Shawn Inmon
Enumclaw Washington,
July, 2013

Please enjoy a Sneak Peek into to
Feels Like the First Time:
A True Love Story

Prologue
February 10th, 1979

Dawn was at the side of the room, crying softly. I didn't want to see her tears, but I couldn't stop looking at her. I knew I might never see her again.

I needed to concentrate, but I couldn't focus. Maybe it was the fact that I hadn't slept in two days, or maybe I already knew how this was going to turn out. Either way, I couldn't follow what everyone was saying.

Dawn looked questioningly at her mom, who nodded her permission. She came and stood behind me, placing her hand on the back of my neck. When I felt her gentle touch, I couldn't hold my tears back anymore.

I realized it was quiet and everyone was looking at me. I took the wad of bills out of my jeans pocket and laid it on the table.

"I know you've told me I can never see Dawn again, but I can't agree to that. I will agree not to see her for three years, but she'll be an adult then and she can see me if she wants."

"Fine," said Colleen, eyeing me with contempt. It was clear she wasn't worried about Dawn wanting to see me in the future.

"That's it then," I said softly, almost to myself. There was nothing left to say. My composure was completely gone. Hot tears ran down my face, but I didn't care. This was the moment I had done everything to both cause and avoid. It was possible I might see Dawn again at some future date, but I would never see this Dawn. She was so lovely it broke my heart to look at her.

I went to her and put my hands on her shoulders. I looked deeply into her eyes. I didn't ask her to wait for me. I was trying to set her free.

"When we can see each other again, if you still love me, I'll be there for you. I promise I'll love you just the same."

She nodded. Her tears ran like a faucet and she looked away.

I walked out of her house, across the familiar yard and into the rest of my life.

Where True Love Goes
December 1st 2006 - 8:03 PM

It had already been a very long day, but I wasn't in any hurry to get home to Enumclaw. As I drove north on I-5, I turned the volume up on the CD I had just bought that day – Yusef Islam's *An Other Cup*.

I was exhausted and unhappy, but that was normal. At 46, I was slowly killing myself by eating too much, not exercising at all, and withdrawing from everyone around me. I didn't much care if I lived or died.

I had been in my second marriage for five years, but it felt more like a prison than a marriage. The divorce I knew was coming was just another in a long string of failed relationships stretching back thirty years.

Four years earlier, I had told my wife, Adinah, that I didn't love her.

"You don't get to do this," she replied. "If you think it changes anything, it doesn't." And so life went on. I had tried to end our marriage ever since, with no success. I couldn't find the emotional strength to get it over with and say the magic words: I want a divorce.

I was still ninety minutes from Enumclaw and realized I was starving when I saw the last Centralia exit in my headlights. I jerked the wheel to the right at the last moment and cut off a gold sedan. I could barely hear the honk of their horn over my music, but I saw the finger, telling me to have a nice day.

I wasn't sure what food I might find on this exit, but when I pulled off the freeway, I instinctively turned left. Up ahead, I saw a sign that read *Bill & Bea's*. I hadn't even known that place was still open. I'd eaten there a lot when I was in high school in the '70's but hadn't been back since I'd moved out of Lewis County.

Shawn Inmon

Without a thought, I eased into the parking lot and got in line behind an old pick-up truck. Yusuf Islam - the former Cat Stevens - was singing that he went where his true love goes. I clicked it off because I didn't particularly feel like listening to that sweet sentiment.

I was beginning to think the truck in front of me was never going to get their order when they finally pulled away, leaving a blue cloud of exhaust in their wake. I pulled ahead and waited to place my order. The girl at the drive-thru window smiled the way pretty young girls do at safe-looking older men. She took my order and disappeared.

A minute later another woman came to the window and asked me a question, but I didn't answer. An electric charge started at the top of my head and ran down my spine. My stomach flip-flopped and my hands went slick against the steering wheel.

I gaped at her. There was something about her, but I couldn't quite grab what it was. Just looking at her made my heart race. She had shoulder-length wavy auburn hair and soft features with brown eyes that jumped out at me. Her face swirled through my memory, but wouldn't come into focus.

"I just need to know if you want onions on your chicken sandwich," the woman repeated patiently.

I couldn't answer. My brain was stuffed with cotton.

"Yes, please," I finally mumbled. As she walked away, I thought maybe she felt something unusual too. But after a brief pause, she was gone.

Why were fireworks going off in my head? Who was that woman? She was attractive, but I see attractive women every day without acting like a fool. From the drive-thru window, I could see her standing next to a flattop grill talking to the girl who had initially taken my order. The woman laughed suddenly and a thunderbolt hit me. I had never been able to forget those laughing brown eyes.

Dawn.

I hadn't seen her in 27 years, but I knew it was her. I watched her slide gracefully between the counter and the grill to pick up an order. My mind wandered through long-buried memories I thought would never resurface.

She had lived for so long only as a memory; it was exhilarating to be so close to her again. As the years and decades

193

passed, I came to believe I would never see her again. I accepted that, and even found odd comfort in the sense of closure. Finding her so unexpectedly sent my head spinning. She brought the bag with my food. She took my money and handed me change with a tiny smile, but no hint of recognition. I wondered how she could not recognize me. She thanked me and turned away, but I couldn't let her vanish again.

"Did you go to Mossyrock High School?"

I took my foot off the brake and the car eased forward slightly.

"Yes."

"Class of '82?"

"No. '81."

Of course that was right. I was terrible at math under pressure. Her dark eyes focused intently through the drive-thru window. She put her hand on her hip and cocked her head slightly to the right, trying to place me.

"We went to school together."

She stared blankly, and I couldn't take the suspense. I gave her my biggest smile. "Dawn, its Shawn."

She was quiet for a moment.

"Shawn who?" she finally asked.

The question took the air out of my ego. I wondered if I really looked so different. She examined me and I could tell she wasn't making the connection.

"Shawn Inmon. We lived next door to each other." I thought of adding, "You know - your first?"

She took a half-step back with stunned recognition. Her hands flew to her mouth and her brown eyes widened. It was a gesture the years never washed from my memory. I watched her expression flood with memories.

"Oh my God," she said. She paused and said it again. Each word was its own sentence. The young girl who took my order bounced over with a broad smile.

"Hi!" she said. "I'm Connie, Dawn's daughter."

I offered a lame smile to Connie. It was impossible for me to look away from Dawn. I laughed nervously but couldn't speak. Ten seconds of awkward silence followed as a Buick idled patiently behind me.

"I'm Shawn," I said weakly to Connie. My eyes were trained

on Dawn. "Your Mom and I were friends a long time ago." Connie's smile told me she knew what kind of friends we had been. Dawn simply murmured, "oh, my, God" over and over, shaking her head. She chanted eerily, like a record needle stuck in a groove.

I tried to say something to break through, but I was so stunned at being this close to her, I couldn't think of anything.

"It was good to see you", I mumbled. "I was just on my way home to Enumclaw". Dawn didn't seem to hear me. She was lost in her own world.

I grew frustrated at my inability to get my brain and tongue to work together. I turned to Connie.

"Tell your Mom it was good to see her, okay?" I gave her a poor attempt at a wink and failed. I took one last, long look at Dawn, and drove off, dizzy with the thought of her.

I wanted so badly to turn my car around and run into the tiny restaurant, yelling, "Dawn. Baby, it's me." I wanted to hold her tight against me and let the intervening years evaporate. Discretion and the ring on my finger prevailed, and I kept my wheels rolling forward, moving me further away from her with each second.

I had suppressed all thoughts of her for three decades. Now she was real again, and I couldn't prevent the surge of feelings. Memories, sensations, and emotions swept over me in relentless waves, choking me as I merged onto I-5.

The years had changed nothing. I loved her still, infinitely, after so much time. I loved her as I had when I kissed her tear-stained face goodbye on Valentine's Day, 1979.

I turned my music up and let the miles roll under my wheels. My body was in 2006, but my mind, spirit, and heart were firmly lodged in the 1970's.

Purchase in paperback and Kindle at Amazon.com
http://www.amazon.com/Feels-Like-First-Time-Story/dp/1479258946/ref=sr_1_3?s=books&ie=UTF8&qid=1373303484&sr=1-3&keywords=shawn+inmon

About the Author

Shawn Inmon is originally from Mossyrock, a very small town in rural Washington State. He used Mossyrock as the setting for both *Feels Like the First Time* and *Both Sides Now*

He has been a real estate broker in Enumclaw, Washington for the last twenty years. Prior to that, he worked as a short-order cook, travelling T-shirt salesman, radio DJ, Cutco Cutlery sales rep, department store buyer, video store manager, crab fisherman, Kirby vacuum cleaner salesman, business consultant and public speaker. Shawn has often said that he learned everything he needed in life by having 400 different jobs.

He married his high school sweetheart Dawn thirty one years after he first asked her for her hand. Together, they have five daughters, five grandchildren, two chocolate labs named Hershey and Sadie and a crazy flame-tipped Siamese named Buddha.

If you'd like to see pictures of the people and places Shawn wrote about in *Both Sides Now* and *Feels Like the First Time,* please visit the photos page on his website: ShawnInmon.com/photos

If you'd like to know when Shawn has a new book coming up, you can sign up for his New Release Newsletter here: http://eepurl.com/vS7Rn

Shawn would also like to invite you to drop in at his Facebook page: http://Facebook.com/shawninmonwriter

Finally, if you'd like to send Shawn a message directly, his email address is ShawnInmon@gmail.com. He'd love to hear from you.

And on a personal note, Shawn would like to say: *Thank you so much for taking the time to read my book.*

Made in the USA
San Bernardino, CA
08 November 2013